Reconsidering John Calvin

Randall C. Zachman places Calvin in conversation with theologians such as Pascal, Kierkegaard, Ezra the Scribe, Julian of Norwich, and Karl Barth, and attends to themes in Calvin's theology which are often overlooked. Zachman draws out Calvin's use of astronomy and his great concern to see ourselves in comparison to the immensity of the universe, acknowledging in wonder and awe our nothingness before God. Throughout, Zachman presents a Calvin who seeks a route out of self-deception to self-knowledge, though Kierkegaard shows that it is love, and not judgment, that most deeply reveals us to ourselves. The book discusses Calvin's understanding of the election of the Jews, and their relationship to God, and further reconsiders Calvin's understanding of judgment, and how the call to love our neighbor is undermined by the formation of alliances.

RANDALL C. ZACHMAN is Professor of Reformation Studies at the University of Notre Dame. He is the author of *Image and Word in the Theology of John Calvin* (2007), *John Calvin as Teacher, Pastor, and Theologian* (2006), and *The Assurance of Faith: Conscience in the Theology of Martin Luther and John Calvin* (2005). He is also the editor of *John Calvin and Roman Catholicism: Critique and Engagement, Then and Now* (2008) and, with Howard P. Louthan, of *Conciliation and Confession: The Struggle for Unity in the Age of Reform, 1415–1648* (2004).

CURRENT ISSUES IN THEOLOGY

General Editor:
Iain Torrance
Princeton Theological Seminary

Editorial Advisory Board:

David Ford   *University of Cambridge*
Bryan Spinks   *Yale University*
Kathryn Tanner   *University of Chicago*
John Webster   *University of Aberdeen*

There is a need among upper-undergraduate and graduate students of theology, as well as among Christian teachers and church professionals, for a series of short, focused studies of particular key topics in theology written by prominent theologians. *Current Issues in Theology* meets this need.

The books in the series are designed to provide a "state-of-the-art" statement on the topic in question, engaging with contemporary thinking as well as providing original insights. The aim is to publish books which stand between the static monograph genre and the more immediate statement of a journal article, by authors who are questioning existing paradigms or rethinking perspectives.

Other titles in the series:

RANDALL C. ZACHMAN

Reconsidering John Calvin

CAMBRIDGE
UNIVERSITY PRESS

CAMBRIDGE UNIVERSITY PRESS
Cambridge, New York, Melbourne, Madrid, Cape Town,
Singapore, São Paulo, Delhi, Tokyo, Mexico City

Cambridge University Press
The Edinburgh Building, Cambridge CB2 8RU, UK

Published in the United States of America by Cambridge University Press, New York

www.cambridge.org
Information on this title: www.cambridge.org/9781107015753

First published 2012

Printed in the United Kingdom at the University Press, Cambridge

A catalogue record for this publication is available from the British Library

Library of Congress Cataloguing in Publication data
Zachman, Randall C., 1953–
Reconsidering John Calvin / Randall C. Zachman.
    p.   cm. – (Current issues in theology)
Includes bibliographical references and index.
ISBN 978-1-107-01575-3 – ISBN 978-1-107-60177-2 (pbk.)
1. Calvin, Jean, 1509–1564.   I. Title.
BX9418.Z34 2012
230′.42–dc23
2011038184

ISBN 978-1-107-01575-3 Hardback
ISBN 978-1-107-60177-2 Paperback

This book is dedicated to the memory of my parents,
Anne Gaylord Morley Zachman
and
John Wesley Zachman

Contents

Abbreviations

CD   Karl Barth, *Church Dogmatics*, ed. G. W. Bromiley and T. F. Torrance (London and New York: T. & T. Clark, 2009).

CNTC   *Calvin's New Testament Commentaries*, ed. David W. Torrance and Thomas F. Torrance (Grand Rapids, MI: Eerdmans, 1959–72).

CO   *Ioannis Calvini opera quae supersunt omnia*, ed. Wilhelm Baum, Edward Cunitz, and Eduard Reuss (Brunswick: A. Schwetschke and Son (M. Bruhn), 1863–1900).

CTS   *The Commentaries of John Calvin on the Old Testament* (Edinburgh: Calvin Translation Society, 1843–48).

LCC   *Calvin: Institutes of the Christian Religion*, ed. John T. McNeill and translated by Ford Lewis Battles (Philadelphia: Westminster, 1960).

OE   *Ioannis Calvini Opera Omnia, Series II, Opera Exegetica Veteris et Novi Testamenti* (Geneva: Libraire Droz, 1992–).

OS   *Ioannis Calvini opera selecta*, ed. Peter Barth, Wilhelm Niesel, and Dora Scheuner (Munich: Chr. Kaiser, 1926–52).

Introduction

The opportunity to reconsider the theology of John Calvin was presented to me by the gracious invitation to give the Warfield Lectures at Princeton Theological Seminary in October of 2009, in honor of the five hundredth anniversary of Calvin's birth. I am deeply grateful to Dan Migliore and Elsie McKee, who extended this invitation to me. I was encouraged to create lectures that were both historical and constructive in nature, so that I might develop themes in Calvin's theology in light of my own contemporary theological concerns. The idea I had for the lectures was to bring the theology of Calvin into dialogue with the claim that God is love, which is slightly different than Calvin's understanding of God as the author and fountain of every good thing. I also wanted to build on Calvin's claim that the goal of our knowledge of God is to be ravished with wonder before the beauty, majesty, and goodness of God, for this wonder reduces us to nothing, and thus provides the best foundation for genuine and profound humility before God. Thus my goal in reconsidering John Calvin is to develop his insights into the knowledge of God and ourselves in light of the understanding that God is love, to provide a fuller understanding of the humility before God to which Calvin summons us, a humility that is ultimately produced by wonder.

I have chosen six themes in Calvin's theology, and have brought them into conversation with other theological voices, in order to create an irresolvable dialectic at the heart of all six themes. The way this dialectic is developed differs in each chapter. In the first chapter, we explore Calvin's passionate interest in the contemplation of the universe by astronomy, in light of his claim that "astronomy is the alphabet of theology." Calvin thought that our contemplation of the works of God should always begin with the heavens, as this presents the clearest image of God in the universe. Such contemplation is directly related to the theme of humility, for we come to a profound sense of our own nothingness by contemplating the immensity of the heavens, and also come to a clear image of the infinity of God by the near-infinity of the heavens we behold. Calvin's insistence that we be ravished with wonder by the beauty of the universe we behold is rendered dialectical by introducing the voice of Blaise Pascal, who knew through his use of the telescope that the universe is not only beautiful, but it is also terrifying. However, both the beauty and the terror serve to make us more humble, as we realize that we are both at home and lost in a universe of unimaginable immensity and mystery.

In the second chapter, we explore Calvin's increasing appreciation for the image of God that remains in every fallen human being, and the way he appeals to the image of God to develop his understanding of our love for others, including those we consider to be our enemies. Calvin's understanding of the image of God is shown to have two distinctive trajectories, one leading to our loving all people equally, without distinction of friend and enemy, male or female; and the other leading to our loving the saints in the Church more than we love those outside the Church, owing to our being drawn by the exceptional gifts of God we see in them. I develop the former understanding of love with the help of Søren Kierkegaard, in order to show how love does not arise from what we see in our neighbor, but rather from a spring hidden in the human heart that flows from the love that is God. We truly learn to love others by first loving God, so that we can love each person individually, yet no one exceptionally, in light of the God-given distinctiveness of every individual. Such love always leads us outside of the self-love of the alliance, which is created by what we think we behold in the beloved, so that love growing out of the image of God is seen to be both the bond and the critique of all social union.

The next two chapters explore Calvin's understanding of the love of God for Israel, for the Jews, both before and after the coming of Jesus Christ. In the third chapter, Calvin's understanding of the irreducible election of Israel is shown to conflict with his understanding of the Jews as the reprobate people of God. Calvin attempts to solve this dilemma by speaking of an elect remnant of Jews hidden in the midst of the reprobate people of the Jews. Karl Barth is brought in to create the unresolved dialectic of the Jews as elect even in light of their rejection of Christ, so that the whole people is elect even though they do not believe in Christ. However, this position is seen to be unsatisfactory, as it necessarily portrays the Jews negatively, by the shadow cast by their rejection of Christ, and not positively, in light of the inviolable love of God for them.

In order to come to a more positive assessment of the irreducible election of the Jews, I turn in the fourth chapter to another theme in Calvin's theology, the signs of the presence of God in Israel, beginning with the exemplary signs of God's presence in the exodus from Egypt, and culminating in the signs of God's presence in the Temple in Jerusalem, for all of these signs constitute God's eternal pledge to love the children of Abraham. Over against Calvin's claim that these signs cease to have meaning after the coming of Christ, who is God manifested in the flesh, I introduce the figure of Ezra the Scribe, to show how the presence of God is seen to be inextricably tied to the teaching and observance of the Law of Moses after the return from Babylon. This then creates the unresolved dialectic of the need for Christians to acknowledge the loving presence of God in the elect people of the Law, even though they never have and never will accept the preaching of the Gospel.

The fifth chapter examines the different ways Calvin sought to bring each of us to the knowledge of ourselves in light of God's judgment of us, so that we voluntarily confess our sin and nothingness before God. All of these attempts culminate in our being summoned alone in conscience before the judgment seat of God, for this alone is said to lead to the voluntary confession of our own nothingness, which is the heart of our humility. Søren Kierkegaard is brought in again to show how Calvin's objective is best reached by placing us each in silence and solitude before the love of God, for the unresolved dialectic of love is revealed by its being our greatest terror as well as our greatest comfort. The love that makes us out of nothing into something also summons us to become nothing in relation to it, so that God might become everything in us.

The sixth chapter demonstrates how Calvin consistently highlights the love of God by placing it within the horizon of the wrath of God, out of Calvin's conviction that we only know love if we know and experience God's wrath, not only towards ourselves as forgiven sinners in Christ, but also towards the reprobate, whom God created in order to unleash the full flood of God's vengeance against them. This pervasive horizon of wrath and vengeance is challenged by the visions of Julian of Norwich, who was not able to see wrath in God, even though she remained convinced of the judgment of God. The love that is God, which is shown to Julian, creates the unresolved dialectic of hoping for all others, and fearing for myself, for it is my own wrath and anger that forms the greatest threat to my relationship with God and others. In a way, the final chapter represents the golden thread running throughout the book, as it directly challenges Calvin's assumption, seen throughout the previous themes, that the love of God is best revealed against the horizon of God's wrath.

In the final chapter, I return to all six themes of the previous chapters in order to explore further the direction in which I would take each theme, and seek to answer some of the questions that my treatment of each issue raises.

The lectures that form the basis of this book were presented live, without a manuscript, using only an outline and notes. The book itself is based on a verbatim transcript of those lectures, and this transcript has been edited as lightly as possible, in order to preserve the oral character of the reflections. It is my hope that this would not only make the book of interest to those interested in Calvin's theology, but would also make it accessible to those who are interested in the themes discussed in the book, even if they are neither theologians or even Christians. I would like to thank Martina Mullen for her diligent work in transcribing these lectures.

1 | The beauty and terror of the universe: John Calvin and Blaise Pascal

The subject of this chapter is Calvin's understanding of the universe, and we will consider what he says about the stars, the planets, and the sun. This was an area of passionate interest to Calvin, and so I want to consider what he thought about this issue, and why he thought about it the way he did. I am especially intrigued by the phrase he uses in which he describes astronomy as "the alphabet of theology." I would like to explore why he says this, and the various dimensions of that statement. I will then bring in Blaise Pascal, who points out, that with the invention of the telescope and the microscope, the universe is not only beautiful, which Pascal always thought it was, but is also terrifying. That may also explain, I think, why this theme has virtually disappeared in theology. I actually find it intriguing that there are two Frenchmen, Pascal and Calvin, who are theologically interested in the universe, and I cannot really think of anyone else.

So to begin, I have first to create space for this issue in Calvin. One of the most hotly contended issues in Calvin scholarship concerns whether, in fact, the self-revelation of God the Creator in the universe is available in any kind of way to human beings after the fall of Adam. Calvin does not seem to be terribly optimistic at times when he talks about this issue. Echoing Paul in 1 Corinthians 1, Calvin says, "This magnificent theater of heaven and earth, crammed with innumerable miracles, Paul calls 'the wisdom of God.' Contemplating it, we ought in wisdom to have known God, but because we have profited so little by it, Paul calls us to the faith of Christ, which, because it appears foolish, the unbelievers despise."[1] So it seems that the self-revelation of God in Creation would have been something from which we could have profited by contemplating it, but because we profited so little by it, Paul calls us to the preaching of Christ, which we regard as foolish. This, in fact, is the rhythm of Calvin's thought, that he passes from the knowledge of God the Creator to the knowledge of God the Redeemer, and uses this text in the *Institutes* as his transitional text, 1 Corinthians 1.

However, Calvin always had in mind, I would argue, that believers are to move from their faith in Christ back to the revelation of God the Creator because their faith in Christ now reveals to them who the Creator is and what that Creator is like. They now have the eyes to see what they beforehand could not see. Calvin says, "Yet faith in Christ does not prevent us from applying our senses to the consideration of heaven and earth, that we may then seek confirmation in the true knowledge of God."[2] So Calvin was convinced that what we have come to know of God in Christ, we have confirmed by what we know of God in Creation. Calvin always wanted believers to hold these two things together, for the God we see in creation is the same God that we see in Christ, and these two revelations mutually confirm and mutually reinforce each other.

Moreover, Calvin thought that God did us a lot of favors helping us to see this, not only by sending Christ, but also by giving

---

[1]   Inst. II.vi.1, *Ioannis Calvini opera selecta*, ed. Peter Barth, Wilhelm Niesel, and Dora Scheuner (Munich: Chr. Kaiser, 1926–52), vol. III, 320, lines 29–33; hereafter references are in the format OS III.320.29–33; *Calvin: Institutes of the Christian Religion*, ed. John T. McNeill and trans. Ford Lewis Battles (Philadelphia: Westminster, 1960), 341; hereafter references are in the format LCC 341.

[2]   Comm. Genesis Argumentum, *Ioannis Calvini opera quae supersunt omnia*, ed. Wilhelm Baum, Edward Cunitz, and Eduard Reuss (Brunswick: A. Schwetschke and Son (M. Bruhn), 1863–1900), vol. 23, 7–8; hereafter references are in the format CO 23:7–8; *The Commentaries of John Calvin on the Old Testament*, 30 vols. (Edinburgh: Calvin Translation Society, 1843–48), vol. 1, 64; hereafter references are in the format CTS 1:64.

us spectacles, my favorite image. Now that I have presbyopia and I cannot read anything in front of me, this is an image of which I am especially fond. Calvin describes the natural world in our fallen state as a beautiful volume, which we can see without our spectacles, and we know it is some sort of writing, just as I know that the book before me is some sort of writing, but I cannot read it. In both cases, I know something is being communicated to me, but I cannot see it properly. So I need Scripture, which acts as spectacles to clarify this beautiful volume, which I otherwise cannot read. Once I have Scripture, I can suddenly see what it is that is being communicated to me. I think that is actually a beautiful image or metaphor. He uses it in the *Institutes* and in his Genesis commentary because it conveys the fact that people do know that something is being conveyed in creation. There is something being communicated, but they just cannot make it out, and so there is a lot of conjecture as to what it could be, but once Scripture is given, you can see what is right in front of you. He says, "For by the Scripture as our guide and teacher, God not only makes things plain which would otherwise escape our notice, but almost compels us to behold them, as if he assisted our dull sight with spectacles."[3] I like that, "as if he almost compelled us to behold them," in other words, LOOK! It is not just that you could look if you want to, but LOOK! And now you can see.

Calvin thinks that God does some corrective surgery in our eyes, as well. God gives us what Calvin calls "the eyes of faith," so there does seem to be some sort of retinal problems in our eyes along with our need for corrective lenses. And so believers, he thinks, who have the Holy Spirit, and who are united to Christ, actually have the eyes that can behold what is going on in the works of God in front of them and within them. He says, "The world is rightly called the mirror of divinity. Believers, to whom God has given eyes to see, discern the sparks of his glory as it were shining out in every individual creature. The world was founded for this purpose, that it might be

---

[3] Comm. Genesis Argumentum, CO 23:9–10B; CTS 1:62.

the theater of divine glory."[4] That is a very famous line. So the theater of divine glory was founded so that we would contemplate it with our eyes and come to know God through it, and believers now have no excuse. They have faith in Christ, which yields to them the one true God, the fountain of every good thing; they have the spectacles of Scripture, so they can make out what is in front of them; they have the eyes of faith, so that this can penetrate into their inner self, and so they should spend their lives contemplating this image. He says, "Therefore, as soon as the name of God sounds in our ears, or the thought of God occurs to our minds, let us also clothe God with this most beautiful ornament, the universe. Finally, let the world become our school if we rightly desire to know God."[5] As I have argued in several of my works, this theme in Calvin is absolutely essential to him. You cannot be a faithful person, you cannot be a godly person, you cannot be a pious person, and not contemplate God's self-revelation in creation.

But what was it in particular that Calvin wanted us to regard? What were we supposed to contemplate in particular? Calvin says, "The Lord manifests himself by his powers, the force of which we feel within our self, the benefits of which we enjoy."[6] So what we are to behold in the works of God are what Calvin calls "the powers of God." These are often translated as "the perfections of God." We often discuss them as attributes of God. But I think it is significant that Calvin calls them powers because powers work on us. Powers are forces which we experience so that they are not just attributes that could be ascribed to God in an abstract manner, but are actually things that are revealed in what God does, that convey God's nature to us. God's nature, then, actually acts upon us. It is not very remote

---

[4] Comm. Hebrews 11:3, *Ioannis Calvini Opera Omnia, Series ii, Opera Exegetica Veteris et Novi Testamenti* (Geneva: Libraire Droz, 1992–), vol. 19, 184; *Calvin's New Testament Commentaries*, ed. David W. Torrance and Thomas F. Torrance (Grand Rapids, Michigan: Eerdmans, 1959–72), vol. 12, 160.

[5] Comm. Genesis Argumentum, CO 23:7–8C; CTS 1:60.

[6] Inst. I.v.9, OS III.53.14–16; LCC 62.

at all. It is quite intimate. Of these powers in particular, Calvin's three favorite are wisdom, goodness, and power. There is a lot of discussion of these attributes or perfections of God in Calvin, and many scholars seem to think that Calvin was a very anxious person. This is very popular these days. Calvin is an anxious person! So he is portrayed as looking around for something to allay his anxiety, and he seizes on divine power. He wants something really powerful to take his anxiety away, so he wants power, and that makes him feel safe, that makes him feel secure. That, actually, is the last thing that Calvin would ever say. Power by itself, he thinks, is absolutely terrifying, and if all we know of God is power, we are lost. We are crushed. It just reduces us to nothing.

So Calvin always wants to frame the power of God in the context of the wisdom of God and the goodness of God, as well as the justice of God, the mercy of God, the eternity of God and the life of God. We will see many of these powers in this chapter, but I think it is especially interesting that Calvin focuses on the wisdom of God. He is very interested in the wisdom of God, as the wisdom of God is the disclosure of the goodness of God, and the goodness of God is undergirded by the power of God. But what we will see is that the power of God always supports what the wisdom of God is doing, while the wisdom of God discloses the goodness of God, and the goodness of God discloses God. There has been a lot of interest in Calvin regarding these attributes, perfection, powers, and the like. But I want to argue that he does not just look at power. Power to him is absolutely terrifying. Power is important, but in the context of wisdom and goodness, so those are his three favorites. The three are suggestive of the Trinity to him. He will ascribe goodness to the Father, who is the fountain and author of every good thing, including the fountain of divinity within the triune relations; wisdom to the Son; and power to the Spirit. You can see that these three powers always work together. They are never found in separation, so you never have a power that is not wise or a goodness that is not wise, or a goodness that is not powerful. He does not always, though, reduce the three to triune relations, and of course, you could not really do so, because the Son is also good and powerful and the Spirit is also wise and good. But he still likes those three in particular. So he says, for instance, "This, indeed, is the proper business of the whole of our lives in which we should daily exercise ourselves to consider the infinite goodness, justice, power, and wisdom of God," see, there are four now, "in this magnificent theater of heaven and earth."[7] So it is to these powers in particular that he wants us to attend, and you can see justice is in there, so it is not always just wisdom and goodness at that point.

The goal of this consideration, which will be a refrain of these chapters, is to become ravished with wonder and astonishment. I found this theme to be absolutely charming when I first came across it; I thought that he just got carried away one day when he was writing this commentary or something. But this theme occurs over and over again for him. The goal of our knowledge of God and the goal of our contemplation of creation, and especially the goal of our contemplation of the stars and the planets and the sun, is to become completely overwhelmed with awe, with astonishment, and with wonder, so that we can no longer even speak at the culmination of this experience. In other words, you know you have experienced these powers of God, you know that you have experienced the self-revelation of God in your contemplation, when you are completely ravished outside of yourself in wonder, and are reduced to silence. But it is a silence beyond language – it is not a silence before language, it is a silence beyond language. And I find it absolutely amazing that this is Calvin's piety. You are seized outside of yourself by what you see, and you are rapt outside of yourself – that is what the Latin would actually mean – you are taken outside of yourself in wonder, astonishment, and awe. So he says, "As soon as we acknowledge God to be the supreme architect who has erected the beauteous fabric of the

---

[7] Comm. Genesis 2:3, CO 23:33A; CTS 1:105–6.

universe, our minds must necessarily be ravished with wonder at his infinite goodness, wisdom, and power."[8]

Calvin was quite serious about this kind of contemplation. He thought that we should do this every minute of every day. At all times, you should be contemplating the powers of God at work around you and within you. You should be experiencing these powers, you should be enjoying these powers, and you should be rapt outside of yourself in wonder. Of course, he knows none of us do this, which is why he thought that God instituted the Sabbath. And he thought this commandment, this part of the Sabbath commandment, was absolutely binding on Christians. This comes up in a charming exchange between the minister and the child in Calvin's 1545 Catechism. (By the way, on his deathbed, Calvin admitted to poorly writing only one work, which was this Catechism. He was very happy with everything else that he wrote, but he said, "I really never got the Catechism right." And you will hear in this exchange, that the child sounds like a tenured professor, but it is charming.) So the minister says, "But what is the meaning of the Lord exhorting us by his own example to rest?" and the child says, "When he finished the creation of the world in six days, he dedicated the seventh to the contemplation of his works. To incite us the more strongly to this, he sets before us his own example, for nothing is more to be desired than that we should be formed to God's image," which I think is quite significant. The minister says, "But our meditation of God's works is to be continuous. Is this sufficient that one day out of seven be devoted to it?" The child answers, "It is right for us to be employed in it every day. But because of our weakness, one special day is appointed."[9] So Calvin thinks the child is quite right. You can hear the minister, "That is quite right!" I find those exchanges to be really charming. But I think that it is significant that he actually

---

[8] Comm. Psalm 19:1, CO 31:195B; CTS 8:309.

[9] *Catechismus Ecclesiae Genevensis*, OS II.103.13–22; *Calvin: Theological Treatises*, trans. J. K. S. Reid (Philadelphia: Westminster Press, 1954), 112.

stops the Catechism to discuss this issue. The default position is that we should be doing this all the time, so why just one day? And the minister says well, because of our weakness, we should do this at least one day a week. But if we do not do this, we are not imaging God. If we do not do this, we are not like God because God contemplates God's works, and so should we. That is really his point. That is his exhortation. I think this is quite significant for Calvin and he thinks this is actually something Christians should do once a week. And I wonder, What happened? Where did this deep concern to contemplate creation go? I never heard about it when I was younger. It really is interesting that it is so important to Calvin that we contemplate creation, and yet we do not seem to have done a very good job on that.

Moreover, Calvin gave a great deal of thought to *how* we should do this. He was a person who was very conscious of order, the order of teaching, as well as the order of contemplation, and with regard to the latter he always has us begin with heaven. God's works are done all around us; God's works are done within us. He thinks that even if you are blind, you can still feel the life of God within you. You can feel the power of life within you, and that life within you is God within you. Calvin knows that Plato says this, but he thought God inspired Plato to say this to shame us into realizing that this is true, that our very life comes from God, and that we can all feel this life within ourselves. So in a sense, Calvin wants us to see these powers in everything we experience, in everything around us. But he knows us, and knows that this is very difficult to do, especially as we look at human history. Human history is incredibly confusing and problematic and disturbing and troubling and terrifying, and so he thought that you really have to give some attention to where you begin. How do you begin this contemplation that you are to do every day, or at least once a week? You start at night. The first thing you do is you contemplate the heavens. He always comes around to this. My question is basically why, so I am going to try to play out why he does this.

In a relatively astonishing section in the *Institutes*, Calvin summarizes how we are to appropriate the knowledge of God the Creator. And he is talking now about the godly. What are we supposed to do with this knowledge? How are we supposed to make it our own? He says:

> Therefore, let the reader understand that he or she has a genuine apprehension of the character of God as the Creator of the world. First, if you attend to the general rule, never thoughtlessly or obliviously to overlook the glorious powers which God displays in God's creatures. And second, if you make an application to yourself of what you see, so as to fix it deeply in your heart.[10]

So what you contemplate should affect you deeply, you can see that rhythm again. And then he talks about what we should contemplate in the works of God. He said the former – "never thoughtlessly or obliviously to overlook the glorious powers of God" – is exemplified "when we consider how great the architect must be who framed in order the multitude of the starry hosts so admirably that it is impossible to imagine a more glorious sight, so stationing some and fixing them to particular spots that they cannot move," so we can see the physics are very different, "giving a freer course to others, setting limits to their wanderings, so tempering the movement of the whole as to measure out day and night, months, years, and seasons, and at the same time so regulating the inequality of days as to prevent everything like confusion."[11] There is no confusion. And then we contemplate God's power in sustaining so great a mass. He says that these few examples sufficiently explain what is meant by recognizing the divine powers in the creation of the world. He is done. All he has talked about is the starry host. All he has talked about is the positioning and the movement of the planets and the stars, the sun and moon. And he thinks that is sufficient. I think that is really interesting. And actually I never noticed that before, that all

---

[10] Inst. I.xiv.21, OS III.171–72, LCC 181. [11] Inst. i.xiv.21, OS iii.172.4–13; LCC 181.

he mentions is the heavens. I was going to move on to how it is sup-posed to deeply affect us, but it is quite significant, I think, that he stops at this point. So he wants us to start with the glorious powers of God at work in the heavens, and in this instance, he does not go any further than that. So I think this actually indicates how passion-ately Calvin thought about this.

Calvin is also aware that there are various ways in which we can contemplate the heavens. There is what everyone can do – and you all should be doing this, by the way, every week, at least, if not every day – and that is to walk outside and look at the sky. Of course, we all cannot do this, as Calvin could, because of ambient light. And I think this is really quite something, actually, Calvin would consider this to be a tremendous loss, that human beings have succeeded in securing their lives at night to such a degree that they cannot even be awestruck by the sky over them. They have a chance every day to be completely overwhelmed by the majesty of the stars and the planets, and yet now this contemplation is blocked for most of us. If you have ever seen a map of the United States at night, it is really astonishing. I remember my wife and I were up in the Adirondacks last winter and it was this icy, cold night, when you walk out in the snow it goes *crrk, crrk, crrk*, like that, it's very crunchy, and we went out to the lake, which was quite expansive, and then we just stood there and we looked up. And there was no humidity, there was no ambient light, nothing, and you just feel yourself *phooshh*, you know, it's just like you're gone. So this is what Calvin had in mind. And imagine him in the sixteenth century at night looking up at the sky. It must have felt like the Milky Way was right there for him to touch. So he thinks everyone *can* do this, and everyone *should* do this. You don't have to be smart. You don't have to be educated. You don't have to know how to read. You haven't read anything. You don't know anything. You can do this. You *should* do this, and you will get enough out of it by doing that. I think that's interesting. So he says that even the most illiterate peasant – and illiterate was not meant by him as an insult because he tried to teach people how to read – can see enough of the starry host to come to an understanding of the powers of God and the existence of God being revealed thereby.

But Calvin is also aware of what he calls "natural astrology." Now it's one of those things that happens in terms of names, that eventually, to distinguish the Nancy Reagan kind of astrology – and I don't mean to make fun of that, because actually Martin Luther and Philip Melancthon were deeply interested in the Nancy Reagan kind of astrology – natural astrology was given the name of astronomy. We now call it astronomy, but in Calvin's day it was called astrology. So all of it was astrology, the study of the stars. But Calvin is aware that there are people who have dedicated their lives to deeply studying this subject, to studying the stars, to studying the planets, to studying eclipses, to studying comets. There is a long history, going back really to human prehistory, of interest in the stars. Stonehenge comes to mind. Calvin did not know about it, but he would not be surprised at all by it, actually. The people he knew, especially, were the Egyptians on the one hand, and the Babylonians on the other. If you read any history of astronomy, they are very significant stations along the way. These people undertook learned investigations of the universe. They were not just contemplating it in an unlearned way, they were studying it. And Calvin commends them for this. He says, "Anyone assisted and enabled to attain a deeper insight into the secret workings of divine wisdom cannot be condemned." This is actually a good thing. He says:

> To investigate the motions of the heavenly bodies, to determine their positions, measure their distances, and ascertain their properties, demands skill, and a more careful examination; and where these are so employed, as the Providence of God is thereby more fully unfolded, so it is reasonable to suppose that the mind takes a loftier flight, and obtains brighter views of his glory.[12]

---

[12] Inst. I.v.2, OS III.46.16–20, LCC 53.

But then he comes back to say that even the common folk and most untutored can contemplate the excellence of the art of divine wisdom. But he really is aware that there are people who have studied this much more deeply than others, and he does not want them condemned. He does not want them ridiculed or left aside because they are learned and because they are elites, basically. He thinks there is something to commend in this. He thinks we can learn from these studies even if we ourselves cannot do them. He even says in his sermons on Job that every believer, even the most unlearned, should be an astrologer. "Let us mark well that Job's intent here is to teach us to be astronomers, so far as our capacity will bear," for "God intends to make us astronomers, so far as each man's capacity will bear it."[13] Whether or not you are an astrologer in the way he's talking about, in this learned way, or are just in the ordinary way, everyone should be interested, passionately interested, throughout their lives in the heavens and the motions of the heavens. So you have this learned investigation and then you have the ordinary comprehension or contemplation.

Calvin was also very interested in the nature of what he calls natural astrology. He wrote a work distinguishing this from what he calls judiciary astrology, which he thinks is the attempt to predict the future very precisely. "You will meet a beautiful woman and she will change your life," that kind of thing. He really did not have any time for that. But he did, in fact, think that this did not mean that the study of the heavens was a waste of time, quite the contrary. "True astrology," notice the same word, "is the knowledge of the natural order and the arrangement which God established for the stars and the planets, which involves estimating their office, property, and power, and subjugating their entire science to God's end and use."[14]

---

[13] Sermon 33 on Job (9:7–15) (Edinburgh: Banner of Truth Trust, 1993), 157A.

[14] *Advertissement contra L'Astrologie qu'on appelle Iudiciare*, CO 7:513–42; Mary Potter, trans., "A Warning against Judiciary Astrology and Other Prevalent Curiosities," *Calvin Theological Journal* 18 (1983), 165.

And he thinks that the main difference is that everyone knows what the *effects* of astrology are, and he thinks in particular of seasons, but not everyone knows their *causes*. By the way, do you know that over half of the college graduates in the United States do not know why there are seasons? They don't. They probably think the way Calvin did, that the sun just goes further away and it's orbiting the earth. I mean, it's very sad to me; such is our ignorance of astronomy now, and our indifference to it. We don't even know what we should basically know ourselves. So one of the things you learn in astronomy – I will just use the word astronomy now to avoid confusion, but he uses astrology – one of the things you discover is why seasons are the way they are, why winter and summer follow each other. So you learn the causes of things, not just their effects. Moreover, he thinks that this study leads to the knowledge of eclipses. Why do lunar and solar eclipses happen? Everyone knows *that* they happen, but they do not know *why*. They don't know what the cause is, and astrologers study the natural causes of natural effects. See? And he thinks this is a very good thing.

When he finally gives his description or definition of astronomy, it is really quite exhaustive. I told my wife I was going to read the whole thing. She warned me it might be a little long, but I think the detail is quite astonishing, revealing just how interested he was in this science. He says, "Thus astrology serves to determine the courses of the planets and stars, as much to discover their duration as their path and position. Astrologers study their duration in order to know what term each planet and the Earth require to complete their circuits." How long does it take them to do their circuits? And remember, for him, the Earth is stationary and everything else is moving. And actually that is astonishing, if you think about it, what it would have meant for that to happen, all of this stuff is moving around us. I think it really is quite amazing. He says:

> They study their positions to know how great the distance is between them, to determine whether their movements are direct, oblique, or

contrary to one another. To be able to demonstrate why the sun is farther away from us in the winter than in summer, and why it stays longer with us in summer than in winter. To be able to use a compass to determine what sign of the zodiac a planet or star occupies each month, and what points of intersection it has with other planets. To know why the moon waxes or wanes as it recedes from or approaches the sun. To understand how eclipses occur, and to be able to mark their position to the last degree and minute on the compass. This foundation laid, we can tell that the effects which we see on earth follow.[15]

So he actually thinks there is a relationship, a natural relationship, between the movements and the positions of things in the heavens, and what happens on earth. In other words, he thinks that the earth is part of the cosmos. He thinks that it is one with everything we see in the universe. And if you see the causes going on there, you can actually conjecture, you can actually follow or extrapolate down to effects on earth. He even thinks it has medicinal uses. For instance, his doctor, Benedict Textor (we know his name, for he even commends his correction of Erasmus' translation of 2 Timothy 4:17), would do bloodlettings for Calvin based on the position of the stars. And Calvin thought this was actually legitimate, that you should be able to do this. And he thought clams were more productive during certain phases of the moon than others. So it's all very charming, but on the other hand, the insight, I think, endures, that we are part of the cosmos. And what happens in the remotest distances of the cosmos affects us, and what happens here affects things there.

Calvin also is aware later in his career, and I think this is quite prescient of him, actually, of the danger that this kind of study presents, namely, the study of the natural causes of natural effects, and he writes a comment about Aristotle's treatise *On Meteors*. He is worried that Aristotle is attempting to create a veil that will conceal

---

[15] Ibid.

the work of God, conceal the powers of God, by accounting for everything exhaustibly by natural causality. So everything that is a natural effect has *only* a natural cause. Calvin thinks that this is the danger of this kind of study: it can attempt to account exhaustively for all of the effects that we see by all the causes that we see. But Calvin does not solve the problem by appealing to miracles. He does not solve the problem by breaking the cause–effect nexus. He does not solve the problem by arguing against Aristotle. He tries to solve the problem by arguing that this whole process of natural cause and effect manifests something vastly beyond natural causes and effects. And the awareness of that, the recognition of that, is wonder. There is not an argument to be made here. It is an appeal to the experience of wonder. You cannot look at these processes and not be astonished. And the *more* you understand them, the *more* you will be astonished. See, that is what he is trying to argue. So he is actually not afraid of these kinds of investigations. He warns us that we should not think we are explaining everything by natural causality. But on the other hand, he wants to know the natural causes of natural effects. And as you can see, he is up on his game. He gives a pretty good detailed list of what astrology was doing in the sixteenth century. So he seems, actually to have taken a very intense interest in it.

Calvin is also aware, and this is quite amazing to me, that what astrologers or astronomers tell us, is not what the Holy Spirit in Scripture tells us. The Holy Spirit in Scripture tells us that the moon is the second great light. Astronomers tell us that the moon is opaque and reflects the sun, although Calvin thought it was in the sphere of fire, and so it must, even though opaque, have a little bit of light in it. But he knows it is basically opaque. It is not one of the lights like the sun. Moreover, Scripture tells us that the moon is the second largest object in the sky, whereas astronomers tell us that Saturn is much bigger than the moon. Moses tells us through the Holy Spirit that there is water above the atmosphere, and astronomers know there is fire above the atmosphere. (A hundred years from now people are going to be laughing hysterically at what we think is absolutely true.

But more of that when we get to Pascal.) In any case, this creates quite a conflict. And of course, the United States of America has suffered deeply over the past hundred and some years over this conflict. What if the natural investigation of natural causes and effects tells you that the way things work in the universe is vastly different than what Scripture says?

Now you think this would create an insurmountable problem for Calvin, because Calvin is famous for saying something biblical inerrantists love: "Our true wisdom is to embrace with meek docility, and without reservation, whatever the Holy Scriptures have delivered."[16] But instead, at this point Calvin actually completely shifts gears. He says that Scripture is written for unlearned people. In fact, this is one of his mottos. "Scripture is the book of the unlearned." Not images, the way Gregory the Great says, but Scripture. This means that the Holy Spirit and the human authors of Scripture, including Moses, Daniel, Jeremiah, Isaiah, Jesus, and Paul, are writing for people who do not know anything, who are not learned. And you do not show off your knowledge of astronomy when you are teaching that kind of person because they will be totally turned off and they will think, "What a jerk. I don't know what he or she is talking about; I don't have time for this." You will instead tell them things according to the way they experience the world, and you will lead them on from there. You will accommodate yourself to the lowest capacities of your audience, not in a patronizing way, not in a condescending way, but in a respectful way, by engaging people where they actually are.

So the Scriptures, which are the book of the unlearned, do not falsify the inquiries of the learned, for the learned are studying more deeply the powers of God at work in the world, and they are what reveal God to us. Calvin actually distinguishes between the learned investigations of what we would call scientists (he called them philosophers, since there were no scientists at this time), which are true, and the teaching of Scripture, which is accommodated

---

[16] Inst. I.xviii.4, OS III.227.27–30, LCC 237.

to ordinary comprehension and is therefore not learned. He says, "The one who would learn astronomy and other recondite arts, let him go elsewhere [than Genesis]. Here the Holy Spirit would teach all people without exception, and therefore what Gregory declares falsely and in vain depicting statues and pictures, is truly applicable to the history of Creation, namely that it is the book of the unlearned."[17] And he goes on to say that actually Moses knew better. He was convinced that when Moses was being raised in Pharaoh's household in Egypt, he learned Egyptian astronomy. So Moses knows what Calvin knows. Daniel knows what Calvin knows. He was taught by the Babylonians, so he knows Babylonian astronomy. Calvin thought Jeremiah knew this, Amos knew this, and Isaiah knows this. When we look in the prophets we see how often they refer to the stars and the planets, and Calvin makes an interesting point. And so Moses knows better when he writes about the universe in Genesis, but he is teaching people that do not know any better, and he is not going to insult them and bore them and distract them. So he does not tell them these things. But, Calvin says, here is the difference. "Moses wrote in a popular style things which without instruction, all ordinary persons endowed with common sense are able to understand. But astronomers investigate with great labor whatever the sagacity of the human mind can comprehend. Nevertheless, this study," that is, astronomy, "is not to be reprobated." And we know Calvin was not shy about reprobating things, so this is a good thing! He says, "For astronomy is not only pleasant, but also useful to be known. It cannot be denied that this art unfolds the admirable wisdom of God."[18]

The art of astronomy, this learned art, unfolds the admirable wisdom of God. So the more you understand about Creation, the more you understand about the universe, the more you unfold the admirable wisdom of God, and this kind of study is not to be

[17] Comm. Genesis 1:6, CO 23:18C; CTS 1:79–80.
[18] Comm. Genesis 1:16, CO 23:23; CTS 1:86

rejected. He says, to conclude, "If the astronomer inquires respecting the actual dimensions of the stars, he will find that the moon is less than Saturn, but this is something abstruse, for to the sight it appears differently. Moses, therefore, rather, adapts this course to common usage."[19] I find this absolutely astonishing. If people had appealed to this earlier on, because Calvin is one of the very favorites of the anti-science Bible movements, we could have avoided a whole series of conundrums that I think have plagued us, for Calvin is convinced that scientific investigation is very different than Scripture. And it does not mean that Scripture is wrong; it just means we are not to read Scripture to find out how the world works. Why would we ever have done that in the first place? Calvin thinks if you want to know how the world works, check it out! And read the Egyptians and the Babylonians. Okay, and he could have thrown in the Greeks, I don't know why he never does, but he could have thrown them in, but they learned a lot of what they learned from the Egyptians and the Babylonians. So this is very interesting, a science or liberal art that comes from unbelievers is eminently useful for believers because it unfolds the wisdom of God, and it is the wisdom of God for which we should be searching in our contemplation of the universe. And this leads him to make the claim to which I alluded earlier regarding astronomy. Calvin says, "And indeed astrology may justly be called the alphabet of theology. For no one can with a right mind come to the contemplation of the celestial framework without being enraptured with admiration at the display of God's wisdom as well as God's power and goodness."[20] So for him, astronomy, contemplating the heavens, is a fundamental and essential element of theology. And he is talking here, actually, about the Egyptians and the Babylonians, in this context. For Calvin, this science, this learned investigation, this learned contemplation, unfolds the admirable wisdom of God in a way that is absolutely irreplaceable and necessary, making this kind

[19] Comm. Genesis 1:16, CO 23:23; CTS 1:87.
[20] Comm. Jeremiah 10:1–2, CO 38:59A; CTS 18:8.

of study the alphabet of theology. You cannot really be a theologian, you cannot spell in theology, unless you study astronomy.

So my question really is, why? What was it that Calvin saw in astronomy that he didn't see in, say, botany, or that he didn't see in biology or zoology? I mean, these were all in nascent form in his day, but he knew plenty about them, he knew Aristotle and Pliny on these subjects. So why was it astronomy that was the alphabet of theology? Now my wife would say biology is the alphabet of theology, so you know not everyone agrees with Calvin on this, and I would like to sort of puzzle it out for a bit. One of the reasons he thinks this is true has to do with the way the wisdom of God is manifested in the order of the heavens. Calvin is very interested in how the heavens themselves display an order, display symmetry. Mentioning the stars in Isaiah, he states more clearly that "the wonderful order which shines brightly in the face of the heavens preaches loudly that there is one God and creator of the world. And all who shall observe that amidst the vast number and variety of the stars, so regular an order and course is so well maintained, will be constrained to make this acknowledgement."[21] For him there is regularity and an order in the heavens that everyone can see, and this is why astronomy is so important to him, because this order manifests the wisdom of God.

Calvin also distinguishes the order you see in the stars from the order you see in the planets and then in the sun. And remember, everything is moving. Everything is moving. He says, "As to the heavens, what do we see there? An innumerable multitude of stars so arranged as though an army were so in order throughout all its ranks, and then appeared the wandering planets." See, the stars for him are fixed and the planets make their way through them freely, "having each its own course and then appearing amongst the stars. Then the course of the sun, how much admiration ought it to produce in us!" And he says this not only for the learned but for the

---

[21] Comm. Isaiah 40:26, CO 37:25B; CTS 15:232.

unlearned, "for when the sun, in its daily course, completes so great and so immense a distance, they who are not amazed at such a miracle must be more than stupid."[22] So Calvin's amazement is that a body the size of the sun can complete its course in the period of a day, because that is what he thinks is happening. I think, personally, spinning at 29,000 miles an hour is just as amazing as the sun going around the Earth. And so he goes on in great detail about the sun rolling through its circuit, making it a wonderful specimen of God's wisdom. What amazes him in particular is the fact that you have stationary stars and moving objects, like the sun, the moon, and the planets. And yet they do not smash into each other. My wife and I were driving around Princeton, and you all know this better than we do. It is quite astonishing how people drive in Princeton. They think that these are a lot bigger roads than they wind up being, and so the chance of collision is quite great, as we know, when objects are moving. And for Calvin the velocity of these bodies is astonishing. He knows the speeds are incredible, he thinks he is accounting for it by the Earth being stationary, but the speeds really are truly incredible. And so for him the fact that this is all harmonious and this is all orderly manifests the wisdom of God. The power of God is also revealed, because only God could sustain such a machine, and he calls the universe a machine, this incredibly complex, this incredibly orderly movement, but at this tremendous velocity. So he says, "We have a signal proof of the glorious power of God." Notice that is added to the wisdom, "that notwithstanding the immensity of the fabric of the heavens, the rapidity of their motion, and the conflicting revolutions which take place in them, the most perfect subordination and harmony are preserved and that this fair and beautiful order has been uninterruptedly maintained for ages. It is apparent, then, how the ancientness of the heavens may commend to us the singular excellency of the handiwork of God."[23]

---

[22] Comm. Jeremiah 51:15–16, CO 39:454C; CTS 21:220.
[23] Comm. Psalm 68:32, CO 31:635–36; CTS 10:43.

RECONSIDERING JOHN CALVIN

Moreover, this contemplation of the orderliness of the heavens for him is actually the best way to come to an understanding of the Providence of God because God is the wisdom and the power and the goodness governing all of this, and we see a greater order in the heavens than we do anywhere else. So we need to train our eyes by looking at the wisdom of God in the heavens because that will allow us better to see it all around us. And that will allow us to see it, as he says, even in the minutest of plants.[24] So the spectacles of Scripture and the eyes of faith are also strengthened and nourished, if you will, by the contemplation of the wisdom of God in the heavens, so that we can start to see it where we least expect to see it, and that is around us and within our own lives and our own experience. And even, as he says, in the minutest of plants. If I had time, I would talk about how he contemplates the minutest of plants, but unfortunately, I don't. But he wants this contemplation to go on further than the heavens. So the fact that there is this harmony, and there are no collisions, there are no what he calls concussions, there are no disturbances – this for him is incredible. And all of this is moving at a tremendous velocity, so this should just amaze us and astonish us and just take us outside of ourselves. So I think this wisdom and this unsurpassed power of God are very important aspects of why he thinks astronomy is the alphabet of theology.

But there is a further point, I think, than this, and that is that astronomy dislocates us. Astronomy makes us contemplate the vastness of creation, what he calls the near-infinity of creation. When we contemplate the heavens, our earthly, carnal, self-interested, all-too-human preoccupations with the presence of God right here, right now, only with me, are deeply challenged because God is present in the remotest reaches of the universe in the same way that God is present here. God is at work in the remotest stars of the heavens as intimately as God is at work here. God's wisdom, God's power, God's goodness is at work everywhere in the universe, and therefore, here.

[24] Ibid.

I think ultimately this it is why this study is so central to theology and to the lives of the pious, because the heavens are the closest image we have of the infinite nature of God. The universe is not nearly as big to Calvin as it is to us, but I think the same idea would follow. When you contemplate the heavens and the vastness of them – even though they are in spheres moving around the earth, for Calvin they are still incredibly immense – that immensity humbles us in our presumption to think that God is only here where we want God to be. And it also blows through our conceptions that finitize God, that make God a comprehensible, finite thing that we can control.

Theology needs to know this: God runs the universe. God does not just operate according to your ideas, and God certainly is not captive to your ideas or our ideas. God is in control, and when we contemplate that, we lose control. When we contemplate that, we lose the ability even to speak about it, but when we contemplate that, we ascend, he says, as it were by steps, to the knowledge of God. The more incomprehensible the world becomes to us, the more we are approaching just how incomprehensible God is. But it is the incomprehensibility of the self-revelation of God. It is the incomprehensible wisdom of God, it is the incomprehensible power of God, and it is the incomprehensible goodness of God that we are experiencing. And you are seeing it. I mean, just look, you are seeing it right there. So I think that is actually what he is after, why this study is so important for him. He says, "Scripture often teaches that God in is heaven. Not that God is shut up in it, but in order that we may raise our minds above the world and may not entertain any low or carnal or earthly conceptions of him. For the mere sight of heaven ought to carry us higher and transport us into admiration."[25] So the mere sight of heaven just makes you realize, what was I thinking? What was I thinking? He actually has Jeremiah telling the Israelites, you think you have God boxed up in the temple? Guess again. Look at the heavens and tell me God is just in the temple. I mean, it really is amazing.

[25] Comm. Isaiah 66:1, CO 37:436B; CTS 16:409–10.

I think this is very useful advice. So the alphabet of theology, I think, is precisely this awareness of the transcendence of God that we attain through what we can see in the heavens. It is an experience of the infinitude of God through what we can contemplate, and through what we can meditate on, and through what we can even study.

But what we come to know makes our place in the universe very, very tenuous, and it decenters us and it places God, really, back at the center, in a way that Calvin thinks is very salutary. He says, "It could doubtless be that a person would be a thousand times filled with wonder and admiration, for the more carefully we attend to the consideration of God's works, we ourselves, in a manner, vanish into nothing. The miracles which present themselves on every side before our eyes overwhelm us."[26] So I think ultimately that is why Calvin wants us to study the heavens. Calvin thinks that in astronomy, whatever form it takes, just looking at the sky in a contemplative way, not just looking up, but contemplating it, in an ordinary way, or learning more about it and investigating about it more fully in a learned way, the ultimate goal is to be ravished in astonishment and reduced to nothing. But it is a nothingness of wonder, it is a nothingness of astonishment, it is a nothingness in the face of God's glory. I really do think that for him this is the goal. He says at one point, "The contemplation of the works of God ought always to end with wonder."[27] And the wonder really is the sense of being snatched outside of yourself in awe and simultaneously being reduced to nothing.

The question becomes, and this is where I'd like to turn now, what happens to our contemplation of the universe, and what happens to our experience of ourselves as members of the universe, when we take the spectacles of Scripture and the eyes of faith, and add to them the telescope and the microscope? This actually happens in the time of Galileo and the time of Pascal. What is amazing to me about

[26] Comm. Jeremiah 51:15–16, CO 39:454C; CTS 21:220.
[27] Comm. Psalm 139:13, CO 32:381B; CTS 12:214.

THE BEAUTY AND TERROR OF THE UNIVERSE

Pascal writing in the 1650s is that he figured out what this meant, so that you could apply his insights to the time of the Hubble telescope, and I think you basically have the same story. In fact, in some ways I think Calvin fits in pretty easily to this time as well. But I posed the question earlier, why is it that this theme in Calvin, about which he was so insistent in the *Institutes*, in his commentaries, in his Catechism, has virtually disappeared? Where did it go? Why don't people who claim to follow Calvin's teaching actually follow his advice to study the heavens? You cannot really follow Calvin and not do this. He was adamant about it. He had to be an astronomy nut, you know, he wants us lying on your rooftops every night being swept away in amazement. So what happened? And I think part of what happened is Calvin's own sense that our wonder will reduce us to nothing, and we don't like that especially much, and it will reveal the infinitude of God compared to our own earthly conceptions of God, and we don't like that very much either. But the other reason is what Pascal saw as he looked through his telescope. Calvin at least thought that the machine of the universe had an order and symmetry to it and we knew where we were. We were in the center, which actually for him, as for ancient physics, is the lowest part. Most people think the world at the center of the universe means it is the most important. It is actually the garbage heap of the universe, for all the crud settles in the middle. The apex of the universe is the stars, for the stars are nearly eternal, and are qualitatively different than the earth. When Dante ascends from Mount Purgatorio looking in Beatrice's eyes, he goes through the planetary spheres to the celestial spheres and that ascent brings him closer to God. So the earth being at the center of the universe does not mean it is the most important, it actually just tells you that you are at the bottom, but at least you know where up is. And Calvin does think that the heavens are closer to God than the earth, and they more clearly reveal God than the earth does.[28]

[28] Comm. Psalm 19:1, CO 31:194C; CTS 8:308–9.

But Pascal, by his own investigations with the telescope, knows that there is something terribly different now. There is no "there" there anymore. We do not know where we are anymore. And we still don't. So Pascal says at one point, regarding a thoughtless person who denies religion:

> When I see the blind and wretched state of humanity, when I survey the whole universe in its dumbness, its silence, and humanity left to itself with no light, as though lost in this corner of the universe, without knowing who put us here, what we have come to do, what will become of us when we die, incapable of knowing anything, I am moved to terror, like a person transported in sleep to some terrifying desert island who wakes up quite lost and with no means of escape. Then I marvel that so wretched a state does not drive people to despair. [29]

See, we are lost in some corner of the universe. Actually, it is worse. We are lost somewhere in the universe. There is no corner in the universe, okay? The earth is rotating at 29,000 miles an hour; the sun is traveling through space at a tremendous velocity, as well. The Milky Way, we came to know very recently, is traveling at one million miles an hour, and will eventually, they think, collide with the Andromeda Galaxy. So much for harmony and symmetry, and no concussion! But even though Pascal was looking through a refractor telescope of the kind Galileo and Kepler used, and not the reflector telescopes we use today, he still knew we were lost, he knew we did not know where we are anymore, and he could not believe that this did not bother people. They were not concerned about this. They did not think about it. And we don't either! This is true! We are hurtling through space, and we don't know where we are going, influenced by forces that we do not understand at all. And yet, we do not even think about it.

So Pascal is very helpful, actually, in diagnosing why it is we ignore this, for once we consider our place in the universe, it is terrifying

---

[29] Blaise Pascal, *Pensees*, trans. A. J. Krailsheimer (London: Penguin Books, 1966), 88.

THE BEAUTY AND TERROR OF THE UNIVERSE

as well as awesome, it is frightening as well as wonderful. He says, "I see the terrifying spaces of the universe hemming me in, and I find myself attached to one corner of this vast expanse without knowing why I have been put in this place rather than that, or why the brief span of life allotted to me should be assigned to me one moment rather than another."[30] Why now? Why here? Where are we going? How did we get here? And this is for him cosmological; this is not just because he is confused. This is what he knows. He knows this in 1650. What do we know in 2009? The things we know in 2009 change every day. Astrophysics gets rewritten every day, and it gets more intense, and ever more awe-inspiring. We now know that the universe is 13 billion years old, and 156 billion light years in size, and growing every second. I read a history of astronomy in which an astronomer finally admitted, by the way, that we have *no idea* what a "light year" means. We just say that, but what does it mean? How far does light travel in a year? Can you imagine that? And what is a billion, by the way, let alone 156 billion light years? See, that is the size of the cosmos now.

Pascal sees our current dilemma very clearly. What we know of the universe is simultaneously as terrifying as it is awe-inspiring. And it is deeply threatening because we just do not understand our place in it anymore. Pascal tries to get his readers to see this by inviting us to contemplate the visible world. He points out that the whole visible world, everything we can see, is an imperceptible dot in the universe. "The whole visible world is an imperceptible dot in nature's ample bosom. No idea comes near to it. It is no good inflating our conceptions beyond imaginable space. We only bring forth atoms compared with the reality of things."[31] See, even the perceptible universe is an atom in the entire universe. This is an amazing insight; I think he is right, actually. I think he got it. But that is terrifying because of what it means when I look at myself. Look at me! I am just this tiny little dot in this perceptible universe that is an atom

[30] Ibid., 158.   [31] Ibid., 89.

compared to the whole. I am swallowed up beyond nothingness by this infinity. But then he says he now wants us to look in the other direction. Now he wants you to approximate not infinity but nothingness. He wants you to look through a microscope, and when you look through a microscope you will see universes within universes within universes in tiny, infinitesimal things. We are finally about to spin microscopic particles at a velocity approximating the speed of light in an accelerator under the mountains of France and Switzerland, in the hope that we can discover the tiniest of the tiniest of things, as they were at the beginning of the universe. Pascal doubted we could ever do this, because for him the minutest things just become another universe and within them lies another universe, and suddenly we human beings appear to be colossal. Suddenly you cannot figure out how we do not just fall through the atomic structure around us.[32]

And so our nothingness in the face of the infinity of the universe becomes our colossal scale before the nothingness below us, and this, of course, is our dilemma. We are caught in the middle of things, moving endlessly between nothingness and infinity. Indeed, we have been thrown from nothingness toward infinity, but we are neither nothing nor infinite, so we cannot touch the bottom and we cannot touch the top. And this for Pascal is why human knowledge is so fragile, why human knowledge is so precarious, why the presumption of human beings to know is so ridiculous. He is writing during a time, by the way, when people are writing encyclopedias, and some of them claim to include the knowledge of everything. And Descartes wrote a book called *On the First Principles*. Pascal thought this meant on the first principles of everything, which would mean that you think that reason touches the bottom and the top, and we simply cannot do that. "For after all, what is humanity in nature? A nothing compared to the infinite, a whole compared to the nothing. A middle point between all and nothing. Who can follow these

---

[32] Ibid., 90.

astonishing processes?"[33] I think this is actually a form of humility, a form of what one might call epistemic humility, to which Calvin himself, I think, would have been sympathetic, but from which maybe at times he could have benefited. I think we *all* could. I think we all talk about things without realizing that we have absolutely no idea what we are saying. And we say these things as though we are absolutely certain of what we are saying. But physics tells us in a way that Pascal would completely understand that we now know maybe 5 percent of the universe – of all that could be known, we know 5 percent. That is astonishing to me, when you look at the way physics works. It is absolutely astonishing that we only know 5 percent. And for Pascal you see this is exactly where we are now. It is not surprising to him at all because if you are between the infinite and the nothing, and are floating between the two equally distant from both, then you really do not know much of anything. He says:

Such is our state. That is what makes us incapable of certain knowledge or absolute ignorance. We are floating in a medium of vast extent, always drifting uncertainly, blown to and fro. Whenever we think we have a fixed point to which we can cling and make fast, it shifts and leaves us behind. If we follow it, it eludes our grasp, slips away, and flees eternally before us. Nothing stands still for us. This is our natural state and yet the state most contrary to our inclinations. We burn with desire to find a firm footing on an ultimate, lasting base on which to build a tower rising up to infinity, but our whole foundation cracks, and the earth opens up into the depths of the abyss.[34]

So I think that our drive to have an infinite ground for what we know that will sustain us and hold us and preserve us is still here, it is a desire that we all have. And we also know now, I think, that we are incapable of finding this kind of ground, because we know deep down that we are floating in a medium of vast extent, blown to and fro.

[33] Ibid.   [34] Ibid., 92.

I do not think that this realization takes anything away from Calvin's insight, that this medium of vast extent is awe-inspiring. It still is beautiful. It is splendorous, it is magnificent – but it is also terrifying. Our world keeps moving, keeps constantly shifting, and we do not really have a way of catching our bearings. I think all of that is salutary for us. I think knowing this actually brings us closer to God rather than further away, but it is an intimacy based on genuine, existential, ontological humility, which gives us an inner sense of our nothingness, and yet of our everythingness. I mean, it makes everything infinitely important even though things are infinitely unimportant. So these are my thoughts. I have, by the way, no solution to this dilemma for us. I think it may explain, though, why we do not think about it. I personally find it very, very haunting. And on the other hand, in a very salutary way, the more I personally think about this, the more it actually opens me up, the more it actually makes me wonder in this kind of genuinely deep way, and the less concerned I become with what used to preoccupy me earlier in my life, namely with getting everything right. You know, we tend to think, especially in theology, that if we are not right, the universe ends tomorrow. But this is why we need astronomy as the alphabet of theology, because we cannot get it right most of the time, and yet the universe is not going to end tomorrow. There is a God at work in the universe, sustaining it and ordering it in astonishingly wonderful and terrifying ways, and all we can do is to lay our lives in the hands of this God. That is what trust is, that is what faith is – laying your life in the hands of that Creator, in light of the magnitude of that Creator's work.

2 | The bond and critique of all social union: John Calvin and Søren Kierkegaard on the image of God

In the last chapter we examined the image of God in Creation, especially the image of God in the heavens, and now in this chapter I want to consider Calvin's thoughts about the image of God in humanity. Calvin gave a great deal of thought to this issue, and it is one of the issues on which he changed his mind considerably during his career. He was very interested in this issue from the very beginning. There were other theologians at the time, like Martin Luther, who were not all that interested in the image of God in human beings. So this is a distinctive theme in Calvin that he pursues his whole life. We will be exploring how he describes this image and the role it plays in undergirding or supporting our love for one another and especially our love for the enemy. This chapter will focus on the love of the enemy in particular but also the love of all other people as kind of a litmus test.

To begin with Calvin's original position on the image of God, which remains throughout his whole career, Calvin insisted that every human being was meant to be created in the image of God, and of course Adam and Eve were the original exemplars of this image. By this he meant that human beings shared in a superlative way in the powers of God about which I spoke in the previous chapter. So we were like God more than any other aspect of Creation. We shared in God's goodness, we shared in God's life, we shared in God's wisdom, God's power, God's justice … and so if Adam had persevered in this image, Adam would have ascended from temporal life to eternal life without experiencing death. Death for Calvin, then, becomes the major sign that the image of God has been fundamentally altered and distorted. So humans shared in the powers of God, which really express the nature of God, and they were meant by that sharing to strengthen these gifts more and more within themselves, to become more and more like God, so at the end of time, they might actually pass from time to eternity and be united to God. This remains the goal of human life for Calvin throughout his career. Human beings were created to be united to God, and we are united to God by becoming like God in God's image when we see God face to face. He says, "The highest human good is therefore simply union with God. We attain it when we are brought into conformity with his likeness."[1] When we become more and more like God we become more and more united to God until finally we are united to God completely.

But of course, we know the story in the garden has a very sad and tragic ending. For Calvin, Adam and Eve were meant to be, if you will, the fountain from which this image was to flow to us. All the benefits which God gave Adam and Eve were meant to flow from them to us. And what happened was that by their sin, especially their unfaithfulness, they lost these good things for themselves and also, therefore, for us. So everything we were to receive from them is gone and cannot be found again until you come to the humanity of Christ. You can see how Calvin's Christology then functions, namely that Christ as a human being contains in himself all of the good things that we lost in Adam, for we need access to another human being who can give us these things. So Christ's humanity becomes the fountain of all good things that we lost in Adam, and Christ in his humanity becomes the one who transforms us back into the image of God. And we'll see this theme of regeneration and transformation coming back in as we proceed.

[1] Comm. Hebrews 4:10, *Ioannis Calvini Opera Omnia, Series II, Opera Exegetica Veteris et Novi Testamenti* (Geneva: Libraire Droz, 1992–), vol. XIX, 63, lines 17–24; hereafter references are in the format OE XIX.63.17–24; *Calvin's New Testament Commentaries*, ed. David W. Torrance and Thomas F. Torrance (Grand Rapids, MI: Eerdmans, 1959–72), 12, line 48. hereafter references are in the format CNTC 12:48.

But for our purposes, Calvin says that when Adam and Eve fell into sin, the image of God was "obliterated." It was "deleted." I love that, in the age of Microsoft Word. Block, delete, it's gone. So it was deleted, it was obliterated. And nothing remains, he says, except the bare ruins of this former image. And you can see this was in 1536; he is in his most excited moment as an evangelical, so his rhetoric is quite strong. There are passages in Calvin's theology which show that this position is maintained throughout his career, but he does become increasingly aware very quickly that he has overstated the case. There are a number of instances where you can see Calvin backing away from an extreme position first set forth in 1536, and this is one of them. His Catholic contemporaries were quick to point out that he had overstated the loss of the image after the fall. The image of God remains, for even in Genesis the prohibition of homicide is based on the image of God remaining in human beings after the expulsion from the garden (Gen. 9:6). So Calvin actually begins to rethink the role of this image, beginning with his *Catechism* of 1537, hard on the heels of his 1536 *Institutes*, in light of the prohibition of homicide. Calvin says that God prohibits the killing of another human being because another human being is created in the image of God, and so violence against another human being is an assault against God. "If we recall that man was created in God's image, we ought to hold him sacrosanct, as he cannot be violated without God's image also being violated."[2] He reaffirms this later in his commentary on the commandment not to kill, that every homicide is sacrilegious, and is an assault against God. "Undoubtedly God would have the remains of his image" – notice now he is speaking of the image remaining – "which still shines forth in people to continue in some estimation, so that all might feel that every homicide is an offence against him."[3] So Calvin backs off from insisting that the image of

---

[2] *Catechismus, 1538*, CO 5:330A; *Catechism or Institution of the Christian Religion, 1538*, trans. Ford Lewis Battles, in I. John Hesselink, *Calvin's First Catechism: A Commentary* (Louisville, KY: Westminster John Knox Press, 1997), 14.

[3] Comm. Deut. 5:17, CO 24:611C; CTS 5:20.

God is obliterated and deleted, and instead insists that the image of God remains. We still have some lineaments of it, and some outlines of it are left, and we can still detect this image in anyone. So therefore, homicide is prohibited.

By 1539, Calvin begins to see the remnants of the image of God in all humans as undergirding the commandment to love our enemies, as well as Paul's statement that there is no distinction between human beings. There is neither male nor female, there is neither Jew nor Greek, there is neither slave nor free. So he appeals, then, to the image of God to explain A) how we could love our enemies; and B) how there could be no distinction, and therefore, how we are to love all others. He says:

> But I say: we ought to embrace the whole human race without exception in a single feeling of love; here there is no distinction between barbarian and Greek, worthy and unworthy, friend and enemy, since all should be contemplated in God, not in themselves. When we turn from such contemplation, it is no wonder that we become entangled in many errors. Therefore, if we rightly direct our love, we must first turn our eyes not to man, the sight of whom would more often engender hate than love, but to God.[4]

So this is a very interesting position that when you love, when you are called to love other people, you should see all other people as being in the image of God, which means above all else that they are related to God. This is why homicide is sacrilegious. Therefore, you are to see other people not in themselves, but in God, because if you look at other people, they will drive you crazy, and you will not love them. You might be indifferent to them, you might be hostile to them, you might hate them for good reason, you might fear them, but you will not love them. You are to see every person in relation to God, and to love that person because you love God, but you are not to look at the person directly, for the image of God in them means

[4] Inst. II.viii.55, OS III.393–94; LCC 419.

that you are to contemplate them not in themselves but in God. God "bids us to extend to all men the love we bear to him, that this may be an unchanging principle: whatever the character of the man, we must yet love him because we love God."[5] So one of the trajectories he develops out of the image of God is a trajectory in which there is no distinction between people and the love we should have for them. You are not even to think about what the other person is in herself, you are to see her directly in relationship to God, for how you treat that person is directly related to how you relate to God. If you love God, you will love that person in God. You do not see that person in and of herself or himself. Calvin thinks that this is the only way we could love those who are hostile to us or unworthy of our love or ungrateful to us.

Calvin appeals to the image of God in subsequent commentaries to support this view, that love makes no distinction, and especially that there is no distinction between the way we love friend or foe. You are to love your enemies just as you love your friends. He comments on Paul's statement to the Galatians that they are to love their neighbor as themselves, which appears to be a commonplace, if you will, but a commonplace we do not understand very well. The word "neighbor," he says:

> includes all people living, for we are all linked together by a common nature, as Isaiah reminds us, "that you hide not yourself from your own flesh" (Is. 58:7). The image of God ought to be particularly regarded as a sacred bond of union; but for that very reason, no distinction is here made between friend and foe, nor can the wickedness of people set aside the right of nature.[6]

Now what you see in this is clearly that the image of God is being brought in to undergird and support the claim that there is no distinction: we are to love all alike because all are the image of God.

---

[5] Inst. II.viii.55, OS III.394.6–9; LCC 419.
[6] Comm. Gal. 5:14, CO 50:251C; CNTC 11:100–101.

The other theme he brings in, and I'm not sure this is appreciated very often in Calvin, is the idea that you hide not yourself from your own flesh, which comes from Isaiah 58. What we are to see in other people for Calvin is not just the image of God by which they are related to God; we are also to see their flesh, by which they are an image of ourselves. I think this is actually a marvelous way of thinking about human to human relationships, that when you see another person, you are to see your own flesh, as in a mirror. The word "flesh" is quite intentional for Calvin because that is our most vulnerable aspect. It is our most visible aspect, and therefore, I think, our most vulnerable aspect. I ask my students when I talk about this issue to think about how much they have to do before they walk out of their apartment or dorm room. Think about how much you have to do to your own flesh before you let the eyes of other people look upon you. This morning, I crept out of our room in the Erdman Center to get a cup of coffee, knowing I could take the elevator directly to the floor where it was set out, because I had a horrific case of bed hair, but my wife and I love coffee first thing in the morning. So I went sneaking down there, but I had not done the necessary preparations with regard to my own flesh and so I was worried that someone would see me. Luckily, no one did! But you know, we use deodorant now and shampoo and lotions and creams, all these things, just to get our flesh presentable to other people, and Calvin is aware of this.

So when you look at another person and see your own flesh, you are looking at another person as vulnerable as you are. And that is to create a bond of empathy, that they are the same flesh as you. No matter what they look like, they are the same flesh as you. I think that is really a marvelous image. When he comments on this passage in his Isaiah commentary, he says, "here we ought to observe the term flesh, by which he means all men universally, not one of whom we can behold, without seeing, as in a mirror, 'our own flesh.' It is therefore a proof of the greatest inhumanity, to despise those in whom we are constrained to recognize our own likeness."[7] So one trajectory that Calvin uses throughout his career with regard to the image of God that remains in us, is the trajectory, in which there is to be absolutely no distinction between friend or foe, between Gentile and Jew, between male and female, rich and poor, slave and free, agreeable or disagreeable, having good taste or lousy taste. You are to love all because you love God. You are to love all because you see in them your own flesh. And this is a line of thought that he will continue to develop throughout his theological career.

But there is another line he develops at exactly the same time, in 1539, in which he sees the image of God as something that we are to see directly in the other, something that is beautiful, so that when we behold it, it will allure our love for that person, and will thereby cancel out any hostility we might feel toward the other. It will cancel out the animosity. It will cancel out even the unworthiness we might also see in that person. And this is a very different line of thinking, for it claims that my love is rooted in the object of my love. You elicit this love from me because in spite of all the other repellent things I see in you – your unworthiness, or your hatred of me – there is something beautiful that allures me to love you. I have only to behold you in a certain way to see that, and when I do, I love you. Calvin develops this understanding of love more fully than the first one in his own thinking, even though it rather remarkably emerges in the same year as the first, 1539. What I want to do is to explore the tension this second position creates in Calvin's understanding of love, and then bring Kierkegaard in as a critical voice, if you will, to show that only the first position can do justice to the love that can love the enemy as well as the friend. Calvin says, "The Lord commands all men without exception 'to do good' [Heb. 13:16]. Yet the greater part of them are unworthy of it if they be judged by their own merit." I love Calvin; he will often say things that most of us are too

---

[7] Comm. Is. 58:7, CO 37:330A; CTS 16:234.

polite to say. So if you love people based on their merits, good luck, but he says, "Scripture helps in the best way when it teaches that we are not to consider what men merit of themselves but to look upon the image of God in all men, to which we owe all honor and love." In every human being there is something we are to honor and there is something we are to love and we are to attend to that, we are to pay attention to that, we are to look at that. He says:

> Assuredly there is but one way in which to achieve what is not merely difficult but utterly against human nature: to love those who hate us, to repay their evil deeds with benefits, to return blessings for reproaches [Matt. 5:44]. It is that we remember not to consider men's evil intention but to look upon the image of God in them, which cancels and effaces their transgressions, and with its beauty and dignity allures us to love and embrace them.[8]

So there is something I am to see in you that is beautiful, that is alluring, that will overcome all the other things that drive me away from you, that drive me crazy, that may irritate me or make me hostile towards you. I am to look beyond that to something in you that is beautiful, that is divine, that will win me over to love you. This is really very different, I think, than the first model. The question, then, becomes, and this is a question that Calvin tried to answer for the rest of his life, what am I supposed to see? If I am supposed to see something in you, what is that? How do I know that the aspect of you that I am supposed to see is the image of God that cancels everything else out? It takes Calvin quite a while to answer this question, but in 1539 he has no idea. Even later on, in his James commentary, he says, "We confess that the image of God has been miserably deformed," notice not obliterated anymore, but deformed, "but in such a way that its lineaments still appear," its outline, if you will.[9] So an outline of the image of God is still there, but what are we supposed to see of

[8] Inst. III.vii.6, OS IV.157; LCC 696–97.
[9] Comm. James 3:9, CO 55:441B; CNTC 3:292.

it? It is only later as he continues to wrestle with this question that he concludes that the image of God must be the thing that distinguishes us from all other creatures. So the remnant of the image of God for Calvin is reason, but he has a rather comprehensive view of what reason is, and he describes reason in practical rather than speculative ways, as a guide for life. In his comments on Psalm 8, where the Psalmist is speaking about the distinguished endowments that set human beings just below the angels, Calvin sets forth a rather exhaustive list of what these gifts might be. "The reason with which they are endued, and by which they can distinguish between good and evil." See, reason for Calvin is practical, reason tells you what is good and evil so that you will do the good and avoid the evil. "The principle of religion, or the seed of religion, which is planted in them." Calvin thinks that every human being has a sense of divinity, a sense of the numinous, which leads them to worship, even if they don't know what it is they are supposed to worship. They could worship a stick, but they still are led to worship because of the sense of divinity, and this is part of the image. "Their social intercourse with each other, which is preserved from being broken up by certain sacred bonds." So we all relate to each other, even as dysfunctional families still manage to relate to each other in some way. "The regard to what is becoming," decorum, the sense of fittingness. You know, you can see this when you go to a worship service. Do we stand during the hymn or do we sit? If no one really knows what is going on, they all look out of the corner of their eye, because we do not want to stand up when everyone else is sitting. That is exactly what he is talking about; we are given the sense of what is becoming, or what is fitting, and concomitantly, "the sense of shame" when you are embarrassed, when you do something inappropriate or wrong, which guilt awakens in them, "as well as their continuing to be governed by laws." See, that is a rather comprehensive list. He says, "All these things are clear indications of preeminent and celestial wisdom."[10]

---

[10] Comm. Psalm 8:5, CO 31:92B; CTS 8:102.

So the reason, which tells you the distinction between good and evil; the principle of religion, which tells you there is some deity to be worshiped; your social bonds with each other, which continue even in spite of human conflict; the sense of becoming and the sense of shame, which reveal when we have done something wrong; and finally, the laws by which we govern our lives together: these universal endowments show that human beings are still the image of God even though this image of God has been distorted. But his short answer usually is that the lineaments of the image of God are found in reason and intelligence. "For some life appears at least in men, they are endued with mind and intelligence, and so far they bear the image of God."[11]

The interesting thing about reason and intelligence, and the interesting thing about this description of the way we are to love one another, is that there can be more or less reason and intelligence, and if there is more or less reason and intelligence, is there not more or less love? If I see more reason in you, does this not elicit more love from me than if I see less or if I see none? For instance, Calvin thinks that drunkenness is so awful – and he is thinking of Noah in particular – because drunkenness obliterates reason, and therefore obliterates the image of God. Therefore drunks are no longer really the image of God, for the image of God is concealed in them, and that is why you should not get drunk, because by doing so you are concealing the image of God. "For certainly, as far as possible, drunkards subvert their own understanding, and so far deprive themselves of reason as to degenerate into beasts."[12] Other people in particular that he thought did this were those he called the "malicious." We would likely call them sociopaths. These are people who are so exercised in evil that they lose their sense of conscience. "And assuredly it is the climax of all sins that a wretched man, who is abandoned to vice, should extinguish the light of his own reason, and destroy the

[11] Comm. Jer. 10:8, CO 38:69C; CTS 18:24.
[12] Comm. Gen. 9:22, CO 23:151A; CTS 1:301.

image of God within him, so as to degenerate into a beast."[13] We now know that sociopaths can be raised this way and not just develop this on their own. But it is terrifying to Calvin that someone could be so exercised in evil that their conscience no longer says anything before they act and they just do evil because they do evil. They are never restrained by the voice of conscience asking, "What are you doing?" They just do it. And for Calvin these people have obliterated in that way the image of God in themselves, they have no reason anymore. So you can actually have cases where the image of God is gone.

I actually think you see this in the way Calvin talks about his opponents. If he thinks that his opponent is a person lacking in what he calls sound understanding, he talks to them like they are animals. This is an aspect of his rhetoric which has a toxicity that you do not notice because he was such a splendid writer, but he will describe the positions of his opponents as the vomiting of that dog or the bellowing of those swine. He is talking about theologians, he is talking about fellow Christians, but if he does not think they have intelligence, then they are swine. If they lack sound understanding, they are not human anymore, they are not the image of God any-more, therefore he does not have to treat them with respect. So you can see where this is going; there can be less of the image because there is less reason and intelligence. When Calvin thinks that reason is lacking, he is quite clear regarding how he thinks these people should be treated.

The other way in which this works, and I think actually this is more pernicious, but also more human, is that there can be *more* of the image of God. When Calvin thinks of this phenomenon, he thinks of the regenerated in the community he called evangelical and orthodox. Those who belong to Christ are regenerated by the Spirit, and are transformed more and more into the image of God, so much so that you will see something in them which is more beau-tiful, more alluring, and therefore more loveable, than what you see

[13] Comm. Deut. 29:20, CO 25:49C; CTS 5:277.

in other people. You should therefore love them more than other people. This, he says, is the most sacred bond of union that you can have. The unfortunate thing is that a lot of this seems to come from the Gospel of John and the letters of Paul, so I don't think Calvin is just making this up. For instance, when Jesus says that we should love one another, Calvin says:

> Love is, indeed, extended to those outside, for we are all of the same flesh and are all created in the image of God. But because the image of God shines more brightly in the regenerate, it is proper that the bond of love should be much closer among the disciples of Christ. Love seeks its cause in God; from him it has its root, to Him it is directed. Thus, as it recognizes anyone as a child of God, it embraces him with the greater zeal and warmth.

This increase in love is fitting, for it comes from God. Calvin says, "It is the highest degree of love, therefore, that is here described by Christ."[14] And he goes on to say that we are also to love those who hate us. Yes, just in case you forgot, there are strangers, and you should love them; there are those who hate us, and you should love them also; but the most sacred bond is loving those who are regenerated by Christ, loving those in whom the holiness and the righteousness and the mind of Christ are being manifested. So he says, "But everything depends on our love being directed toward God and in our loving every man the more in proportion as he excels in the gifts of God."[15]

If our love for others is based on the image of God we see in them, then where there is more or less image, there is more or less love. In this case there is more of the image in the Church than there is outside of it, so you ought to love those in the Church more than outsiders. And you ought to love those in the Church in whom you discern the excellency of divine gifts more than you love others in the Church.

14 Comm. John 13:34, OE XI.2.133; CNTC 5:70.
15 Comm. John 13:23, OE XI.2.133; CNTC 5:66.

This is clearly Calvin's own inclination. He loves Melanchthon far more than he loves others in Wittenberg, for instance, because of the remarkable gifts of God he sees in Melanchthon. This variation of love comes from God, for these are the gifts of God. They are given to others to allure our love for them, and the greater the gifts that God gives, the more we should love the one to whom they are given. But it is our job to discern those gifts. It is our job to discern this excellence that comes from the Holy Spirit. He says, "There are duties which we owe all men arising out of a common nature, but the tie of a more sacred relationship, established by God himself, binds us to believers."[16] So this is a sacred relationship. And then finally he says, "There is nothing, therefore, which ought to make us seek the friendship of men more than God's manifestation of himself among them through the gifts of His Spirit. This is the highest of all commendations among the godly. It is the most sacred bond of relationship which more than any other binds men together."[17] I have done a chapter on Calvin as a conciliating theologian, in which I described the different levels of friendship he establishes based on the divine gifts he sees in other people.[18] So this is a very important issue for Calvin, of deep personal interest. He thinks about what kind of gifts he sees in others and how much he should love them.

What is interesting to me is that this definition of love, which Calvin is drawing out based on Johannine and Pauline texts, is the same definition that you find in Cicero, whom Calvin read a great deal. Cicero says, "But of all the bounds of fellowship, there is none more noble, none more powerful, than when men of congenial character are joined in intimate friendship. For really if we discover in another that moral goodness on which I dwell so much, it attracts

---

[16] Comm. Gal. 6:10, CO 50:263B; CNTC 11:114.

[17] Comm. 1 Thess. 1:3, CO 52:140B; CNTC 8:334.

[18] Randall C. Zachman, "The Conciliating Theology of John Calvin: Dialogue among Friends," in *Conciliation and Confession: The Struggle for Unity in the Age of Reform, 1415–1648*, ed. Howard P. Louthan and Randall C. Zachman (Notre Dame, IN: University of Notre Dame Press, 2004), 89–105.

us and makes us friends to the one in whose character it seems to dwell."[19] I think this is actually how we all live. We see characteristics in others that we like. We see attributes in others that we appreciate. Maybe we do not have these gifts ourselves and so we want to be associated with them, or we see these gifts in ourselves, and since we like other people who are like us, we are drawn to love them. The more these characteristics are there, the more we are drawn to them, and the closer the bonds of friendship. Calvin thinks that since these gifts are the gifts of the Spirit, this increase of love is a divinely sanctioned phenomenon, rooted in the most sacred bond of a relationship. This is the most exalted form of human love, to be bound together with those in whom we see the excellency of the Holy Spirit. But that quote from Cicero could have been Calvin's comment on the Gospel of John, as they sound remarkably similar. I think that most of us simply live in the Ciceronian way. We are drawn to people based on the qualities we perceive in them, and we are driven away from people in whom we do not perceive those qualities. Other people do not even exist for us if we do not see those characteristics.

But Calvin, to his great credit, sees that there is a problem with this description of love, and so the first model always comes back to haunt the second model. He knows, for instance, that Jesus is directly critiquing the Ciceronian model of loving people based on the excellencies we see in them when he tells us to love our enemies. Indeed, he attributes Cicero's position to the scribes.

> Now the scribes, assessing a man's neighborliness by his particular attitude, denied that one should treat as neighbor any but those whose merits made them worthy of our love, or at least, who could respond to the claim of friendship. This is, no doubt, supported by the common opinion, and therefore, the children of the world are not ashamed to acknowledge their resentments when they have any

19 Cicero, *De Officiis* I.xvii.55.

reason to assign them. But charity, which God commands in his Law, does not regard an individual's merits, but pours itself out on the unworthy, the perverse, the ungrateful.[20]

See, that is remarkable – I will just repeat that line again: "The charity which God commands in his Law," which Jesus is commending in his teaching, "does not regard an individual's merits, but pours itself out on the unworthy, the perverse, the ungrateful." That actually sounds to me like a description of the highest level of love. The highest level of love would not be binding ourselves together by the excellencies we perceive in each other, but would rather be loving those who react ungratefully, loving those who are unworthy, loving those who are wicked, loving those who are hostile.

What I hope to do now is to explore the problems in Calvin's second model of love. What is wrong with our being drawn to love another person by what we see in that person, and how might we better build a foundation for what Calvin wants to do in the first model where this love eliminates all distinction? For it is the first model that describes the highest form of love, when you love your foe as much as you love your friend. And Calvin is right; this is the hardest thing in life to do. It is utterly against nature to do this. But I am convinced that this is Christianity. The call to love our enemies and to bless those who curse us is Christianity. If you get that, you get everything. If you do not get that, if we do not get that – and we don't – then we are still lost. So it is, as I said, entirely to Calvin's credit that he raises this issue, but I want now to appeal to Kierkegaard to see if there is a way of developing our understanding of the image of God that avoids this phenomenon of what I call "clumping together." I think we all tend to do this. We all tend to form what Kierkegaard calls "alliances." And in that sense we tend to resemble overcooked rice. We kind of clump together in these alliances like overcooked rice. So how do we break this rice up so that love can flow more freely?

---

[20] Comm. Matt. 5:43, CO 45:187–88; CNTC 1:199.

Kierkegaard, like Calvin, bases his understanding of our love of neighbor on our kinship to God, on our being the image of God, of our being made in the likeness of God. But unlike Calvin, who does this based on the powers of God – wisdom, goodness, power, justice – Kierkegaard does it by his rather simple definition, which he gets from John, that God is love. This is a commonplace to us; we hear this all the time. Kierkegaard's point is that we do not think deeply enough about what this means, that God is love. That is what we will be exploring. "Just as Christianity's joyful message is contained in the doctrine of humanity's inherent kinship with God, so is Christianity's task humanity's likeness to God. But God is Love, and therefore we can be like God only in loving."[21] Notice that being made in the image of God is a task for me. Being created in the image of God does not tell me about you, it tells me about myself. It is a vocation for me. I become more like God the more I love, because God is love. We will see whether or not this love is elicited based on anything I detect in the object of love or not. But for now, it is very important for Kierkegaard, and I think for Calvin in his first position, that the image of God is a vocation. You are to become like God by loving without distinction, and especially by loving foe as well as friend, for as Calvin says, "no one shall be a son of God if he does not love those who hate him."[22] And Kierkegaard I think just takes this theme directly and runs with it. God is love, and we are like God when we love.

Moreover, Kierkegaard thinks that in every single person, there is a spring coming from this love that is God, and this spring is the source of all love. And so in the human heart there is a fountain of love. In every individual human heart, there is a fountain of love. The source of this love is this aquifer called God. Because God is love, there is love in every human being, and this love flows into

---

[21] Søren Kierkegaard, *Works of Love*, ed. and trans. Howard V. Hong and Edna H. Hong (Princeton University Press, 1995), 62–63.
[22] Comm. Matt. 5:45, CO 45:189; CNTC 1:199.

them, if you will, and through them from God. It is really one of my favorite images. He says, "There is a place in a person's inner-most being. From this place flows the life of love, for 'from the heart flows life.' But you cannot see this place, however deeply you penetrate. The origin eludes you in remoteness and hiddenness."[23] So he thinks that we can never see this source of love within us. The more you dive down to find it, the more inscrutable and mysterious it becomes. And you just never find it. My parents have a cottage on Higgins Lake in Northern Michigan, and it is a spring-fed lake. The state of Michigan, which looks like a glove or a mitten, is almost entirely on top of an aquifer, called the Saginaw Aquifer, which is a huge underground body of water that feeds many of the lakes in Michigan, and it feeds Higgins Lake in a rather remark-able way. I remember when I was a child, my mom said, "Over there, off that point over there is a spring that feeds this lake, and they have tried to find the depth of it. They have sent divers down. They have sent unmanned diving instruments down, but they can-not find the bottom." We used to go in the boat and look into the lake to see if we could see where this spring came from, but all we could see was the reflection of the sky in the deep black water. And that is what Kierkegaard is talking about – if you look in a lake to see where the spring is, you cannot see it. It flows ceaselessly into the lake. Similarly, love flows ceaselessly into your life from God, and although you cannot see from where it is coming, you can feel it coursing through you. Kierkegaard says, "Just as the quiet lake originates deep down in hidden springs no eye has seen, so also does a person's love originate even more deeply in God's love. If there were no gushing spring at the bottom, if God were not love, then there would be neither the little lake, nor a human being's love."[24] So if God were not love, then there would be no love in us. However, the spring of the lake can cease to flow so that the lake dries up; but God's love will never stop flowing because God's love is

---

[23] Kierkegaard, *Works of Love*, 8–9. [24] Ibid., 9–10.

eternal. God is eternally love. And so this spring is eternal life. You can see he is also thinking of the well that Jesus talks about springing up in our lives unto eternal life (John 4:14). So it is this spring of love, then, that makes us like God. It is the capacity to love, the need to love that is given to each and every one of us, which makes us the image of God. And Kierkegaard thinks that this love is given to every single human being. Every single human being. This is not a faith community claim; this is an anthropological claim. He says, "Thus, every human being can know everything about love, just as every human being can come to know that he, like every human being, is loved by God."[25] I think that is really quite a remarkable claim, actually; I hope he is right. So every human being can know about love, for every human being is given love, and therefore every human being can know that he or she is loved by God.

The question is, how do we learn how to love? Where do we learn how to love? Who teaches us how to love? And this is where the problem starts. It is inevitable, but it is nonetheless a problem. We learn how to love from other human beings. Other human beings train us how to love, especially, and we all know this, families. Not just parents, but guardians, grandparents, uncles and aunts, foster parents, the state, whoever is caring for you, teaches you how to love. And think about it, they will reward you when you love them in the right way and punish you when you do not. I remember my mother saying, "You cannot love me and treat me like that!" We all get lessons in how to love from those closest to us, and they will tell us, "That is just unacceptable, that is not the way you are going to love me, you will love me like this." So we have this spring of love welling up in us, and then we learn how to use it, we learn how to deploy it, by loving other people, by loving other human beings. And the mistake we make, which we have to unlearn our whole life if we want truly to love, is that we think that our love is elicited by the goodness of its object. We think that there is something in the other person

[25] Ibid., 364.

that we see, that we prefer, if you will, with which we seek to associate ourselves, and that this is why we love the other person, and this is how we are to love the other person. Kierkegaard sees this, actually, as based on a kind of electing love. We single the Beloved out above all other people, and treat her in a way utterly distinct from the way we treat all others. "That is my mother you are talking about!" See? "You can talk about anyone else in the world the way you want, but that is my mother you are talking about!" Or, "There is no one in this world like my wife. There is no one in this world like my partner." No one exists in the world for my love except her. Or other people may exist for me, but not the way this person does. So we single these people out, based on the unique characteristics we see in them.

This is how we learn how to love. We make a similarity with others based on their dissimilarity with everyone else. The similarity is their bond to me. Their dissimilarity is their uniqueness from everyone else. The people we love are splendid people, not just common or average people – they are wonderful people, they are great people. This is what we call love, according to Kierkegaard. And he actually tries to describe it in other words – namely, erotic love and friendship – to teach us that what we call love is not actually love. He says:

> In erotic love and friendship, the two love each other by virtue of the dissimilarity or by virtue of the similarity that is based on dissimilarity (as when two friends love each other by virtue of similar customs, characters, occupations, education – that is, on the basis of the similarity by which they are different from other people, or in which they are like each other as different from other people). Therefore the two can become one self in a selfish sense.[26]

"Oh, you're from Cornell? Or better yet, Colgate?" (my Alma Mater). Then suddenly there is a bond, for this individual is suddenly bound

---

[26] Ibid., 56.

to me by a similarity that makes her dissimilar to all others. So that is the kind of thing he is talking about. We love others on the basis of the similarity by which they are different from other people, or by which they are like us and thereby different from other people. And the problem with this for Kierkegaard is that this is actually self-love. If I love another person based on the character that is distinctive about them, that I have selected as worthy of my love, as deserving of my attention and respect, if I have singled this out, then I am making that other person another "I," and I am joining them to my "I" as another "I." I must have their similarity and it must make them dissimilar from all other people. By doing this, we form what Kierkegaard calls "alliances," which we mistake for communities of love, but which are really alliances of self-love. "What the world honors and loves under the name of love is an alliance in self-love."[27] So if I am going to form an alliance of professors, then we need to get the graduate students out of here, let alone the undergraduates, let alone the janitor! I am not going to associate with a janitor the same way I associate with a professor! That is a dissimilarity. I do not even see him or her. I see the professor. I see the other I. But that is not love. That is self-love. If the only person in the world that exists for you is another person similar to you, and no one else is visible, that is self-love, that is not love.

And so if love is elicited from us by the characteristics we see in the other, that is simply selfish. We are just loving ourselves through another person. Kierkegaard says, "Christianity has misgivings about erotic love and friendship simply because preferential love and passion, or passionate preference, is actually another form of self-love."[28] We may think that we are reaching beyond ourselves when we love others who are similar to ourselves, but we are really forming larger and larger alliances of self-love, and those outside of these alliances do not exist for us, nor do we exist for them. In light of this rather penetrating insight, I have started to ask myself

[27] Ibid., 119.   [28] Ibid., 53.

the following questions as part of my own spiritual discipline: "Who exists for me, and for whom do I exist?" And concomitantly: "Who does not exist for me, and for whom do I not exist?" A friend of mine and I had a joke that when you are attending a conference, they should have color-coded nametags that tell people whether it is worth their while to try to form an alliance with you, whether you have anything distinctive to offer them. An orange tag would mean that you have nothing to offer, so that no one wastes his or her time by asking you, "Oh how's it going?" You are just an assistant professor, or worse, a graduate student looking for a job! "Ah, forget it! I thought you had something to offer me!" And so maybe the associate professor would have a blue tag, indicating that they are a bit worthier, whereas a full professor would be in red, meaning, you had better come over here. And of course a dean or president would be even better – they would have purple tags!

We have all experienced this in our own ways. You go to a party, you go to a function, you go to a conference, or you go to a lunchroom. You do not exist for these people. They do not even see you. Or they do not exist for you. You do not even see them. You know, what is the name of the person who just came through and set up the microphone? That person is invisible, and if that person calls attention to him or herself, that would be bad, because that person does not exist for us. That person had better not stand up here and try to talk about Calvin or Kierkegaard. And concomitantly, if I arrived in a blue jumpsuit and started setting up the equipment, you would say, "That is not the Warfield Lecturer! The Warfield Lecturer is distinguished. The Warfield Lecturer is singular. The Warfield Lecture is excellent." At least, you know, that is the hope.

So this is the kind of phenomenon Kierkegaard is describing, how we are drawn to the excellence we think we see in others. You see, we want to ally ourselves with this excellence. And once we are in these alliances, people outside these alliances do not exist for us. We do not care about them. As a member of a faculty, I can say that faculty are really good at forming alliances. Faculty care about faculty pay. At

Notre Dame, if you fiddle with faculty pay, the alliance kicks in. "How dare you mess with our pay? That's unjust. We need to take this before the Faculty Senate!" But they will turn the other way with a yawn if the administration were ever to cut the pay or benefits of the staff. They don't care. The cashier, the janitor, the cleaning woman, does not exist for faculty. Faculty exist for faculty. Administrators don't exist for faculty, either. Any of you in administration know this. You are now actually the enemy. You used to be on the faculty and therefore were friends with these people, but now they hate you. Faculty exist for faculty. They don't exist for administrators. They don't exist for parking attendants. They don't exist for ushers. "So, then, this distinguished corruption will teach the distinguished person that he exists only for the distinguished, that he is to live only in the alliance of their circles, that he must not exist for other people, just as they must not exist for him."[29] We form these preferential alliances that are not loving at all; they actually are selfish, no matter how large they may be. And you see the selfishness of the alliance by who does not exist for them. These alliances can be national. They can be international. Doctors without Borders exists for Doctors without Borders, it does not exist for Al Qaeda. And Al Qaeda does not exist for the Roman Catholic Church, and on down the line. So these alliances can be local, national, or international, but no matter how large they are, they are simply alliances in self-love.

So how do we come to the point where we unlearn this selfishness, where we unlearn the love of alliances based on preferential love, and where we start to learn how to love our neighbor? Because loving someone based on what you prefer, loving the professor because he or she is a professor, loving the administrator because he or she is an administrator, is not loving your neighbor. As Jesus says, "Do not even tax collectors do the same?" (Matthew 5:46). Do you really have to learn from God to do that? I mean, everyone does that. So how do we unlearn selfish, preferential love and learn truly

[29] Ibid., 75.

how to love, so that we actually love the enemy in such a way that it is no longer "the enemy" that we love, it is our neighbor? So it is not the enemy that you are seeing anymore, it is your neighbor? That is really the question, but if this is to be the case, then whatever else love is, love must no longer be defined by the object of love. The love must be defined by love. Kierkegaard says this rather elegantly. "Thus the perfection of the object is not the perfection of love. Erotic love is defined by the object. Friendship is defined by the object. Only love for neighbor is defined by love."[30] So what we have to do is come back to ourselves, come back to that spring of love flowing deep inside ourselves, and love out of that, for the love of neighbor is based in love. It does flow outside of us, obviously, but it is not based on what is outside of us. And therefore if the neighbor changes, it does not change the love. The love is still flowing from God, and it still goes to the neighbor as a neighbor. It does not go to the neighbor now as a nice person or a mean person or as a farmer or as a butcher, whatever, it goes to the person as a neighbor because it is flowing from the love that has its eternal source in God.

But there is only one way that Kierkegaard thinks we can learn to love this way, and that is if we love the one who gave us this love in the first place. To love others, we have to start by loving God. It is God who put love in us, and therefore only God can teach us how to love. "What a human being knows by himself about love is very superficial; he must come to know the deeper love from God."[31] So we learn how to love by loving God. We must learn how to love the unseen God, and in that way we will learn to love every neighbor whom we see. "The matter is quite simple. A person should begin with loving the unseen, God, because then he himself will learn what it is to love. But that he actually loves the unseen will be known by his loving the neighbor he sees; the more she loves the unseen, the more she will love the people she sees."[32] But in that sense, you see, our love for others is not immediate, it is not elicited

<hr>

[30] Ibid., 66.   [31] Ibid., 364.   [32] Ibid., 160.

by its object, so that we form this close, tight bond, like rice clumping together, so that nothing exists outside of that clump of rice. The love is actually more independent, if you will; there is more space than that because you love God and through your love for God you love others.

What is remarkable, though, is that for Kierkegaard every person is loved by God, and therefore every person has fundamental equality before God. "In the Christian sense there is equality of all persons before God, and in the doctrine of loving the neighbor there is equality of all persons before God."[33] Every person has this love flowing up within him or herself from God, and every person is loved by God. "Thus every human being can come to know everything about love, just as every human being can come to know that he, like every human being, is loved by God."[34] Therefore, there can be no preference in the way we love others, because every person is equal in relation to God. "Insofar as you love the Beloved, you are not like God because for God there is no preference. Insofar as you love your friend, you are not like God, because for God there is no distinction, but when you love the neighbor, then you are like God."[35] Loving the neighbor comes from our loving God, and when we love God we see that God loves every single human being. God loves every human being, not in a sentimental way, like "God loves everyone," but in a deeply personal and intimate way, for God is the source of the love in every human being. And so if you love God you love your neighbor no matter who he or she is, and you love her or him without preference, as hard as that is. And there is no doubt that this love is incredibly hard for us. "He is your neighbor on the basis of equality with you before God, but unconditionally every person has this equality and has it unconditionally."[36]

I think this issue of the equality of our love is the most difficult issue confronting the Church today, confronting Christianity today. How do we love all people equally? What we try to do is to

---

[33] Ibid., 140.   [34] Ibid., 364.   [35] Ibid., 63.   [36] Ibid., 60.

make them into an alliance. We try to eliminate dissimilarities as much as we can to make everyone as similar as we can, or we try to highlight the dissimilarity and add as many dissimilarities as we can. It reminds me of *Saturday Night Live* parodies of the formation of Democratic Cabinets. How many different varieties of people can you get on the Cabinet? Or on the staff of the White House? By doing so, we actually accentuate the differences, we accentuate the dissimilarities, and think that by clumping them all together we have overcome the problem of our dissimilarities. But we have not, we have simply accentuated the dissimilarities. The answer that Kierkegaard proposes is to love God, and when you love God then you can love every single individual. But as he says, we are to love everyone equally, and yet love each one individually, while loving no one exceptionally. "The equality appears in love's humbly turning outward, embracing everyone, and yet loving each one individually but no one exceptionally."[37] We are called to love each person individually, yet no one exceptionally. In other words, we can never relate to people outside our alliances differently than we relate to the people in them, because love for neighbor means the dissolution of all such alliances. We can never think, as Calvin did, that we are to love "outsiders" with one degree of love while loving "insiders" more intimately, with a most sacred bond of union. For Kierkegaard, that is not love any more, but rather self-love. So you are to love everyone individually but no one exceptionally.

This also solves, I think, the problem with the inclusive community which we are trying to build. There is no such thing as an inclusive community. Communities have boundaries. There is always an outsider. There is always someone for whom the community does not exist, especially non-inclusive people. Intolerant people do not exist for the inclusive community. I go to dialogue after dialogue after dialogue in which the people who really need to be at the dialogue are not anywhere in the room, and they do not exist for

[37] Ibid., 67.

anyone in the room. Those who insist that it is Jesus alone, or the Koran alone, or the Torah alone, are not there. So what is the purpose of the dialogue? Those of us who are there already agree. So we just keep talking to each other about how much we agree, but the people who also need to be there are not there, nor do we *want* them to be there, for their presence would undermine the alliance of dialoguing people we have formed. So how do we do this, you see? For Kierkegaard the key is to see every human being as having a God-given distinctiveness, so that when you love each one individually, you are not loving him or her according to a mathematical formula you have developed, but are loving him or her individually. Is that a rich white person, or is that an impoverished African American person, or is that a rich African American person, and that a poor white person? Whatever the categories may be, such categories do not exist for you. This person in her distinctiveness exists for you, and you love her individually and not exceptionally, but you do see her for who she is because God gives her a unique distinctiveness. "To have distinctiveness is to believe in the distinctiveness of everyone else, because distinctiveness is not mine but is God's gift by which he gives being to me, and he indeed gives to all, gives being to all."[38] You are not supposed to just erase that distinctiveness by means of some abstract and universal understanding of the image of God, or of human equality, or by dissolving the individual into one of the alliances we have created based on human similarities or dissimilarities.

On the other hand, our love is not elicited by the distinctiveness of the individual, because our love for that distinct individual is coming from love. The love is coming from love toward this distinct individual before you, and all of us are these distinct individuals. Try as we may, we cannot hide one another or ourselves in the alliances we ceaselessly create, in our clumps of overcooked rice. We are each uniquely distinct, and we are to respect this distinctiveness

[38] Ibid., 271–72.

because it is God-given, and yet we are to ally with none of it. We do not single out one kind of distinctiveness or dissimilarity and say we are going to form an alliance based on that, because we must always be open to *every* distinct individual. Put another way, loving the neighbor has to do with abiding in the love which flows from God and not getting thrown off by what you are seeing in the neighbor, but seeing the neighbor as the distinctive person she is. "To love the neighbor is, while remaining in the earthly dissimilarity allotted to one, essentially to will to exist for unconditionally every human being."[39]

I think this is impossible to do, but this is what we are called to do, for anything else is not love, but self-love. Yes, it is impossible, yet we are called to do this, for this is what it means to live according to the image of God. I do not think we ever really escape our alliances. In my experience, I am never outside of my alliance, I am never outside of this selfish communion of preferential love, and yet the question Kierkegaard poses bothers me. Who does not exist for me and for whom do I not exist? I think the best that we can do is to be haunted by this question over and over again. Every time we try to solve the problem of the person left out by forming a larger alliance, somebody else is left out. That is not the solution. The solution, I think, is to love everyone individually and no one exceptionally. So the tension we highlighted at the beginning in Calvin's theology is not just an issue for Calvin. Rather, I think Calvin does a marvelous job of highlighting how problematic an issue this is for all of us, and how easily we can forget that we are to love all people without distinction because we love God, and go back to loving the members of our alliances based on our preference for those gifts we treasure the most. So Kierkegaard is a very salutary voice, at least for me, reminding me constantly to ask myself this question: Who does not exist for me, and for whom am I unwilling to exist?

[39] Ibid., 83–84.

3 | The one elect people of God: John Calvin and Karl Barth on the Jews

Our duty to love all people individually, yet no one distinctively, leads to the question of whether God can love one community distinctly, over and above any other community. Can we learn from Calvin how to make sense of the irreducible and irreplaceable love of God for the people of Israel, for the Jews, even in light of the love of God for humanity in Jesus Christ? I owe the impetus for the reflections in the next two chapters to my late colleague, Rabbi Michael Signer. The Theology Department at Notre Dame is a remarkable place, in that they would hire someone like me to teach the major critics of the Roman Church during the Reformation and post-Reformation period, and would also hire deeply committed Jewish theologians to teach theology in the theology department. Rabbi Signer was trained at the Pontifical Institute in Toronto, and was an expert in medieval theology, especially Andrew of St. Victor and the Victorine School. But he was also a very provocative thinker, and I remember talking to him in the hallway once about Jewish–Christian dialogue, and I told him that one reason I really like Calvin is that he provides us with a better understanding of the Jews and the role of the Jews in the Christian–Jewish discussion. And Michael said, "Well yes, he does with regard to the Jews before Jesus, but what did Calvin think of the Synagogue down the street?" This question froze me in my tracks, because I did not know the answer, and it led me to an investigation on this theme, the fruits of which I will be sharing for the next two chapters. So I offer these reflections as a homage to him. I do not know if he would like what I am saying or not, but he actually sent me on this trajectory. So the next two chapters are an attempt to explore what Calvin thinks about Israel, and the problems that I uncover in his thought, followed by the solution to the problem proposed by Karl Barth. In the next chapter I will be going back to Calvin to see if I can develop another trajectory in his thought that allows us to view Israel and the Jews more positively, from the perspective of Christian Scripture. This is one of the most intractable theological problems in Christianity, and the most insoluble, but also the most important.

Calvin was deeply concerned throughout his life, and very disturbed, by any attempt made by theologians, especially the Anabaptists and Servetus in his own day, and Marcion and the Manichaeans in the early church, to divide the Church from Israel. He rejected every attempt to say that the covenant made with Israel for land and family and kingdoms was essentially different than the covenant that God makes with the Christian community in Christ. Calvin argued adamantly that the covenant made with Israel is identical to the covenant made in Christ. Moreover, he argues that the grace of Jesus Christ is offered to Israel from the beginning right up to the time of Christ, and the same grace is offered to Israel that is offered to us in the Church. This is a remarkable claim, and I think the importance of this issue explains why Calvin spent so much time interpreting the Hebrew Bible. If you look at his career, he did commentaries on the New Testament relatively quickly, omitting Second and Third John and Revelation on purpose. But then he started immediately on Genesis, and then Isaiah, and by the time he died, he had done the first six books of the Bible, the Psalms, all the minor prophets, and all the major prophets except Ezekiel, and he was lecturing on Ezekiel when he died. They would carry Calvin from his house up the street to the lecture hall where he was teaching and he would lecture on Ezekiel. We still have the transcripts, in which he would say, "But I am too tired now, I have to continue tomorrow," and he died in the middle of these lectures. So exegeting and interpreting the Hebrew Bible was essential to him, and he thought that the Evangelical Church, which he thought of as the

Catholic Church, needed to take the witness of the prophets, the witness of Moses, the witness of Abraham, as seriously as it took the witness of Paul or the witness of the Apostles. So the engagement with the covenant made with Israel is a constitutive part of Calvin's work as a theologian.

Now Calvin is clearly aware that Christ is never named in the Hebrew Bible. The name "Christ" is, to be sure, for it means "the anointed one." Actually, Cyrus, one of the kings of Persia, is called the Christ (Is. 45:1), but Jesus of Nazareth, the Christ, is never named in the whole of the Hebrew Bible. Of course, this is an interesting problem. Calvin solves this, by the way, by an appeal to an oral tradition that accompanied Israel from Adam to Caiaphas, which told the Israelites that all of these prophecies are really pointing to Jesus, to the Christ that we confess. He realizes that there is no textual basis for his claim, and so in a way this oral tradition has to accompany the law and the prophets all along, to point this out. "But since no clear and, as they say, literal evidence of his death and resurrection exists in the law, there is no doubt that they had teaching handed down by the fathers, from which they learned to refer all figures to Christ."[1] Calvin understands the prophetic foreshadowing of Christ in light of the pedagogy God adopts with Israel. God does this knowing that Israel develops and grows over time, and so like Irenaeus of Lyons and the apostle Paul, Calvin views Israel as a child growing up, and God as a kind of parent/teacher training Israel to grow up in the right way. God wants Israel to grow up into the fullness of Christ, so that when Christ comes, the Jews will recognize Jesus and believe in him as the Christ. So this pedagogy will change over time as the capacities of the Israelites develop, and this is how he answers Marcion. Marcion claims that the God of Israel and the God of Christ cannot be the same God, for the God of Israel delights in punishing and slaying, whereas the God of Christ delights in forgiving and showing mercy. Calvin responds

[1] Comm. Acts 26:22, CO 48:545–46; CNTC 7:280.

by stating that God appears to change because God is just adopting a different pedagogical strategy over time, because the capacities of the people develop over time. God remains the same, but God's approach changes over time.

Calvin was especially interested in the symbols of sacrifice. This is quite understandable given the extraordinary polemic in which he is engaged with the Roman Church over the sacrifice of the Mass. Calvin thought the sacrifice of the Mass, and the ordination of priests by bishops to offer Christ as a sacrifice on altars for the benefit of the living and the dead, was *the* blasphemy of the Roman Church, for it directly denies the benefits won by Christ by his death on the cross. So his interest in Israelite sacrifice is directly related to his understanding of and argument against the sacrifice of the Mass. But it is also directly related to how Christ and Christ's benefits would be offered to the Israelites. And he is actually quite skilled at pointing this out. He wonders, for instance, why Cain and Abel offer sacrifices right after the expulsion from the garden. There is no commandment given by God to offer a sacrifice and yet they offer sacrifices. And it is the blood sacrifice of Abel that is accepted by God. Calvin takes this as a sign that it is blood sacrifice in particular that represents to the ancient Israelites in their childhood the sacrifice of Christ in his death on the cross. There are many other symbols that represent Christ to Israel for Calvin, including Melchizedek, the king priest of God Most High, who is a very important figure for him. By the way, Rabbi Signer just could not figure out why this figure is so important to Calvin. He would ask in exasperation, "What is it with Christians and Melchizedek? I mean, he is mentioned twice. Who is this guy?" Melchizedek is important to Calvin because he is a king and priest in one person, which will not happen again, he thinks, until Jesus Christ. So Calvin understands the whole cultus of the law to be representing Christ, but it was the sacrifices in particular that represented him to the Israelites. Calvin is thinking especially of the statement in the Epistle to the Hebrews, that without the shedding of blood there is no forgiveness of sins (Heb. 9:22). And so the blood sacrifices represent to the Jews the one blood sacrifice of Christ that will be offered once and for all.

Calvin is also very interested in the distinct periods or eras of this economy of the manifestation of Christ to Israel. He makes the claim, which I think is fairly accurate, that once you enter a new era, you cannot go back to the old era. So the initial era of sacrifice is the time of the patriarchs and the matriarchs, during which you could offer a sacrifice to God any time you wanted at any kind of altar you wanted to build. So Abraham builds an altar beneath the oaks of Mamre to offer sacrifice to God (Gen. 12:7). Noah, after the flood, decides to offer a sacrifice to God. He does not need to be a priest; he does not need permission (Gen. 8:20). Calvin again thinks that there is an oral tradition telling them how to offer sacrifice, since there is no explicit command in Scripture. So in the early period, anyone can offer a sacrifice pleasing to God. But when you get to Moses at Sinai, a new dispensation comes in: the Tabernacle is created, and the priesthood is created, and only the priest can offer a sacrifice at the Tabernacle. Once that takes place, you can no longer go off and build an altar somewhere, and offer sacrifices as you wish. When this new era comes, you cannot go back. The third era for this dispensation would be the building of the Temple. In Israel itself, the Tabernacle could travel to various holy sites and priests could offer sacrifice there. Once the Temple is built, according to Deuteronomy, that is the only place you can offer sacrifice (Deut. 12:1–7). Of course, the Northern Kingdom never accepted that claim. Until the Assyrians came and took them into exile, they rejected what they considered to be Jerusalem's ideology, insisting that the original sacrifices were offered up in Bethel and so they would continue to offer up sacrifices there. But there was still the awareness that Jerusalem was claiming itself alone as the site for sacrifice. And Calvin is even aware of how important it was for the Jews when they came back from Babylon to rebuild the Temple, to re-institute the sacrifices. This for him was essential so that Christ could again be represented to the Israelites in his self-offering on the cross.

As the different eras of sacrifice develop, and as the people grow up, Calvin thinks that the representation or the portrait of Christ in these symbols becomes clearer. He has a wonderful illustration of this development that he gets from the Epistle to the Hebrews (Heb. 10:1) that is based on fresco painting. When Michelangelo or someone like that wanted to paint a fresco, they would do a charcoal outline on the wall, and then they would fill it in with color. Calvin sees Christ being portrayed to the Israelites in the same way. At first, all you would see is the charcoal outline, during the era of the patriarchs and the matriarchs. There is a figure being represented there, but it is just an outline. But as time goes on, the portrait gets filled in more and more, as more detail gets added. The coming one is going to be a priest as well as a king in Jerusalem and will be associated with the Temple, so that you start to get a living portrait. The closest living portrait would be Isaiah 53, where Calvin thinks that Christ is being virtually painted to life. So there is a sense in which the Israelites and the Jews, as time goes on, have a clearer and clearer picture of the one who is coming, whose benefits they are already enjoying. The expectation is that this one people, trained and educated by God for thousands of years through a rich array of symbols in the cultus of the law, as well as through the offices of kings and priests, would be able to recognize Jesus when he appeared, and would embrace him as the Christ and Savior. They would see that he matches the prophetic portrait they had been given, and is therefore the fulfillment of the promises, and the reality symbolized by the sacrifices. By contrast, the Gentiles have no pedagogy during any of this time comparable to the one used by God in relation to the people of Israel.

But as we know, this is exactly what does not happen, and Calvin actually seems quite divided about what this means. Why did the Jews not accept Jesus as the one who was being promised to them from the very beginning? And more astonishingly, why did the Gentiles, who had none of this pedagogy whatsoever, embrace Christ almost immediately? Why did the Jews reject him when they had been trained so long to recognize him, and why did the Gentiles, who had not been trained a day in their life, accept him over against the people who rejected him? This development really is the greatest threat to the credibility of the Christian message. That is why this issue is so volatile, and why there is a lot of anti-Jewish thought in Christianity all the way from the beginning. The Jewish rejection of Christ and the Gospel threatens the credibility of the Gospel itself. Calvin actually seems to know this quite directly, since it calls into question his understanding of the essential unity of the Law and the Gospel. He says in his commentary on Romans, "From this, one of two conclusions seemed to follow – either that there is no truth in the divine promise, or that Jesus, whom Paul preached, is not the Lord's Christ who had been peculiarly promised to the Jews."[2] Either the promises to Israel are false or the claims about Jesus are false. That is a pretty stark alternative. Calvin reiterates this threat, saying, "There was no one who would not automatically entertain the thought, 'If this is the doctrine of the law and the prophets, how does it happen that the Jews so obstinately reject it?'"[3] If Christ is the substance of the law and the prophets being offered to the Jews, why do the Jews reject Christ? If the Gospel is a fulfillment of everything that was in the Law, why do the Jews reject the Gospel? It is to Calvin's credit that he sees the seriousness of this issue, and it really is the most serious question that he thought we confronted.

Calvin is clearly of two minds on this issue. On the one hand, he was convinced that by handing Christ over to be killed – Calvin actually says that the Jews kill him, while the Romans seem to disappear – and by persecuting the Apostles, and by trying to silence the Gospel, the Jews are utterly rejected by God, leaving God no other choice but to annihilate them. When Jesus in Luke says, "For there will be then great tribulation and days of vengeance and wrath on that people," Calvin says, "For since the people through obstinate malice had then broken the covenant of God, it was proper that alarming changes should take place by which the air and the earth

---

[2] Comm. Romans 9:1, CO 49:169; CNTC 8:190.   [3] Ibid.

would be shaken. They were rejected by God," he says, and they had to feel and see this for themselves. "Since the Lord executed his vengeance on those men for their inveterate contempt of the Gospel, accompanied by incorrigible rage, let then the Jews' punishment be always before our eyes. Let us learn from it that no offense is more heinous in the sight of God than obstinacy and to spite his grace." And then he goes on to say, "But although anyone who despises the Gospel will be punished, the Jews are punished in a singularly severe way," more than Sodom and Gomorrah, more than the Babylonian exile, more than Assyrian captivity. He says, "that the coming of Christ might be regarded by posterity with greater admiration and reverence, God determined to make a very extraordinary demonstration in the case of the Jews." And then here is where he sums up what God is doing: "For no words can express the baseness of their criminality in putting to death the Son of God who had been sent to them as the author of life. Having committed this inexorable sacrilege, they did not cease to incur the guilt of one crime after another, and thus to draw down upon themselves every ground of utter annihilation."[4] Just as God will not excuse their actions, neither should we. "Yet none of us can excuse the Jews for having crucified Christ, treated the apostles with barbarous cruelty, and for having attempted to destroy and extinguish the Gospel."[5] They are without excuse. None of us should excuse them, and God's vengeance is upon them in a singularly severe way, so that all might learn from this that contempt of the Gospel meets with vengeance. But the vengeance is visited on the Jews with particular harshness and completeness.

It is astonishing, when you think about it, that the very death that was the source of hope for Abel, that was the source of hope for Abraham, that was the source of hope for Moses, that was the source of hope for David, that was the source of hope for Ezra, that was the source of hope for the Jews of Jesus' time, when it actually

[4] Comm. Matthew 24:21, CO 45:660–61; CNTC 3:87.
[5] Comm. Romans 10:2, CO 49:195; CNTC 8:220.

69

happens, winds up bringing wrath on the very people to whom it was promised and symbolized. It is really very ironic, though Calvin never actually caught this irony, that the actual death of Jesus winds up bringing the destruction of the Jews. How could the symbolic representation to the Jews of the death of Jesus bring them hope and forgiveness, if the actual event of his death brings judgment and condemnation? This is something Barth picks up on, as we shall see. But Calvin is quite clear about the calamity that the death of Christ brings to the Jews. In passage after passage, he says, "All hope is taken from the Jews. The divine favor is utterly removed from the Jews." The Jews must be "taught the necessity of their perishing by an inviolable divine decree."[6] He is really quite graphic and quite scathing. "I have no hesitation in stating God's wish to cut off all hope of restoration from the Jews."[7] So this is not just a punishment like the Babylonian exile, which was followed by a restoration; this is the end of the favor of God for the Jews in Calvin's mind. Moreover, when Daniel says, "It shall flow even to astonishment," in terms of God's wrath being poured out, Calvin says that "this slaughter should be like a continual shower, consuming the whole people. "'The slaughter shall flow forth even to consumption,' meaning the whole people should perish."[8] So from the sound of these passages, Calvin's solution to this problem is to claim that God is protecting the truth of the Gospel by destroying the Jews who reject it, by unleashing unparalleled vengeance on the very people to whom Christ was promised, because they rejected him, they rejected the preaching of the Gospel, and they rejected Calvin's doctrine in his own day. "As the rejection of Christ, viewed in itself, and especially as attended by so many circumstances of detestable obstinacy and ingratitude, was worthy of abhorrence above all the sins committed in all ages, so also it was proper that, in the severity of punishment with which it was visited, it should

---

[6] Comm. Daniel 9:26, CO 41:186; CTS 25:222–23.
[7] Comm. Daniel 9:27, CO 41:190; CTS 25:229.   [8] Ibid.

go beyond all others."[9] And so it sounds like God wants the Jews to be utterly eliminated from the face of the earth. These passages are unqualified by Calvin, so it really does sound as though there is no hope at all for the future of the Jews.

Of course, Calvin realizes that there is a problem here, a very serious problem. If the covenant with Abraham becomes null and void, and the promises to Moses and to David and to the Temple are null and void, then we Gentile Christians are completely lost. If the promise to Abraham, to be the God of the children of Abraham forever, can be falsified by human faithlessness, then there is absolutely no promise of God in which you can believe. There is absolutely no faithfulness of God, there is no mercy of God, and there is no promise of God that you can trust. Calvin knows this. So once he has unleashed the severest vengeance of God against the Jews, he has to figure out how the covenant with the Jews can still be in effect, how the promises of God to the Jews can still be valid, how the grace of God can still be present among a people that deserves annihilation. This is the question with which he struggles. When Jesus says, "Unless those days had been shortened, no one would survive," Calvin takes this to refer not to the disciples, which is what many exegetes say, but to the Jews. Unless the days of wrath had been shortened, the Jews would have entirely perished. He says, "Christ presents an appalling view of those calamities," and he is thinking of Titus in particular coming and destroying Jerusalem, "but at the same time mingles it with this consolation: that they would be sufficient to exterminate the very name of the Jews *if God did not look to his elect*, and on their account grant some alleviation."[10] What winds up happening is that in the midst of the Jewish people themselves – and by this I do not think he means the Jews who become Christians; he means in the midst of the Jews themselves – their election will not fail. In the midst of the Jews themselves, who as a people are being destroyed by

---

[9] Comm. Matt. 24:21, CO 45:660–61; CNTC 3:87.
[10] Comm. Matt. 24:22, CO 45:661–62; CNTC 3:87.

God, there is still an elect remnant that will not be destroyed, that is the heir of the promise, that is the heir of the covenant.

> Christ says, that unless God put a period to those calamities, the Jews will utterly perish so that not a single individual will be left, but that God will remember his gracious covenant and will spare his elect according to that other prediction of Isaiah, "Though thy people were like sand of the sea, a remnant only shall be saved."[11]

Calvin's solution to this dilemma is to distinguish between the rejected people of the Jews, and the elect individuals hidden within them as a remnant. On the one hand, Calvin lets the severity and finality of divine vengeance fall upon the Jewish community, so that as a people the Jews are reprobate, as a people they are the special object of divine wrath. In fact, in spite of Calvin's insistence that we cannot know with certainty the election or reprobation of anyone, he thinks that we can know with certainty that God has eternally rejected the Jews. If you want to know who is created by God to be destroyed, it is the Jewish people, after they kill Christ and reject the Gospel. On the other hand, there are elect individuals hidden amongst them, even though as a people they seem to be lost. So Calvin tries to hold together both the rejection of the Gospel by the Jews and the inviolable mercy of God in the covenant made with Abraham, which endures even after the rejection of Christ and the Gospel, by speaking about an elect remnant hidden within the Jewish community itself that endures to this day. He says, "That the covenant should be destroyed by any human unfaithfulness was absurd, for Paul maintains the principle that since adoption is free and founded on God alone and not on men, it stands firm and inviolable, however great may be the incredulity which conspires to overthrow it."[12] So God will be faithful even if we are faithless. God will be faithful to the Jews, not as a people but to individuals, elect individuals. Moreover, those Jews who are being preserved by

[11] Ibid.   [12] Comm. Romans 11:1, CO 49:211; CNTC 8:238.

election are, for Calvin, hidden. They are hidden from view just as the thousands who did not bow the knee to Baal during Elijah's day were hidden from Elijah, leading Elijah to think he was the only one left, as Paul himself says. "For God has a way, accessible to himself but concealed from us, by which he wonderfully preserves his elect, even when all seems lost."[13] So the Jews are not at the end of the day to be despaired of. They are not without hope of restoration; they are not entirely lost as a people. If you are born a Jew it does not mean that you necessarily have to perish. There is, in fact, hope for you because the Church, Calvin says, continues to remain among the Jews. "Although they were unbelievers and had broken his covenant, yet their perfidy had not rendered the faithfulness of God void, not only because he preserved for himself some seed as a remnant from the whole multitude, but also because the name of a church still continued among them by the right of inheritance."[14] This is interesting, actually. Calvin viewed the Church as still being within the Synagogue, for there is present within it an elect remnant, even as the Church is still in the Roman Church, even though deeply hidden from view. There is hope for the hidden elect even in a place where to all appearances there is no hope. Sometimes that election is manifest by individual Jews coming to faith in Christ, but usually not, as otherwise the elect would not be hidden. "Thus general rejection was not able to prevent some seed from being saved, for the visible body of the people was rejected in such a way that no member of the spiritual body of Christ was lost."[15] So then Calvin draws back from his language regarding the complete rejection and extreme annihilation of the Jews. Because of their election, because of their adoption, because of God's promises to them, because of God's faithfulness, the favor of God is not taken away from them, in spite of their blindness, in spite of their rejection of the Gospel. And

---

[13] Comm. Romans 11:2, CO 49:212; CNTC 8:240.
[14] Comm. Romans 9:4, CO 49:172; CNTC 8:194.
[15] Comm. Romans 11:2, CO 49:212; CNTC 8:239.

he really does seem to be quite conflicted about this issue, as you can see, and his feelings run quite hot in both directions.

Calvin also supports Paul's statement that the Jews themselves, going back to Abraham, are the root, whereas the Gentile Christians are the branches. The Jews are the root, and they support the rest of us as the branches. "For he was desirous that the Gentiles should depend upon the eternal covenant of God, in order that they might connect their own salvation with that of the elect people."[16] And so we should not think that we support them or have taken their place or have replaced Israel or have replaced the children of Abraham. They support us. They are the reason we have life. We have been grafted into their root, which is theirs alone. And because of that we have a relationship with God as they do. "It would be unreasonable for the branches to boast against the root, unreasonable that the Gentiles would glory against the Jews, for from the Jews comes their own salvation."[17] This root, this salvation, goes all the way back to Abraham. Calvin thinks that the promise made to Abraham, "I will be your God and the God of your people, of your seed," remains among the Jewish nation today, that God will still be the God of Abraham's people. "If, therefore, it is completely impossible for the Lord to depart from the covenant which he made with Abraham in the words, 'I will be a God unto … thy seed' then he has not wholly turned his kindness away from the Jewish nation."[18] (We will actually speak about this in the next chapter in terms of a possible solution to this problem.) Indeed, in a remarkable passage in the *Institutes* from 1539, Calvin calls us Gentile Christians "posthumous or even aborted children of Abraham" compared to the Jews, who are the legitimate children of Abraham. And by the Jews, he means the Jews who reject the Gospel, like the Jews of the Synagogue down the block, to answer Michael's question. They are the first born in the family of God.

[16] Comm. Romans 11:22, CO 49:223; CNTC 8:252.
[17] Comm. Romans 11:18, CO 49:221; CNTC 8:250.
[18] Comm. Romans 11:29, CO 49:228–29; CNTC 8:257.

Yet, despite the great obstinacy with which they continue to wage war against the gospel, we must not despise them, while we consider that, for the sake of the promise, God's blessing still rests with them. For the apostle indeed testifies that it will never be completely taken away: "For the gifts and the calling of God are without repentance" [Rom. 11:29, Vg.].[19]

So you have a very complex picture in Calvin. On the one hand, it seems as though the crucifixion of Jesus has broken the covenant that God made with the children of Abraham, so that there is now no hope for them any longer. They are completely without excuse, and so God has unleashed severe vengeance on them and will destroy them as a people by an extreme annihilation, beginning with the invasion of Jerusalem by Titus. They are destroyed as a people, they have no hope. On the other hand, Calvin insists that because of divine election and faithfulness, God's blessing is still with them. We must not despise them. The blessing of God still resides with them and will never depart from them. The Church still resides among them, and the elect are to be found among them, though in a deeply hidden way. It is hard to make sense of these apparently contradictory claims. I am going to try to pursue the second line of thinking, regarding the blessing of God remaining with them, in the next chapter, to see whether Calvin might help us see how we might understand the presence of God among the Jews even to this day. But Calvin leaves us with a very complex picture, and some of the passages in his writings are really quite astonishing. I cannot forget especially the one about the Jews laying the grounds for their extreme annihilation. You cannot read that after the Shoah and not almost fall over in dismay. Of course he did not see the Shoah coming, but on the other hand his language definitely did not help.

Calvin solves the problem of the rejection and election of the Jews by having God reject the Jews as a people, so that the Jews as a people

---

19 Inst. IV.xvi.14, OS V.317–18; LCC 1337.

are rejected, are annihilated, are destroyed, while still preserving a hidden remnant amidst this destroyed people, a remnant of blessing amidst this people under wrath. Barth, on the other hand, will not follow this line of thinking. He does not think that Calvin's distinction between a rejected people and elected individuals is legitimate. Barth insists that if the election of Israel means anything, then it is the entire people of the Synagogue, the entire Jewish people, the whole seed of Abraham, that are elected. And they are elected precisely as the people who reject Christ, who reject the Gospel, who have not believed in the past, and will not believe today. As a people, as this people, they are the elect of God. The people of Israel, the people of the Jews, the people of the Synagogue, are the elect people of God. The people of the Jews, in fact, play an irreducibly essential role in God's relationship to all of us in Jesus Christ. If the Jews are not seen as central, then none of the divine promises apply to us. He says, "For the election of Israel occurred for the sake of the Son of God and Man, who is unique, and it cannot, therefore, be surpassed, supplanted or supplemented by any other."[20] That is really a remarkable statement. Moreover, Barth thinks that if you stop hoping for the Jews – and he means by this the Jews who reject Christ, who explicitly say No to the Gospel and go their own way – if you stop hoping for this people, then you cannot hope in Jesus Christ. "Hope in the revelation of Jesus Christ, which is the life of faith, stands or falls with hope for Israel."[21] Thus, if the Church does not see Israel's witness as essential to its own identity, it has abandoned its Lord and Savior. "The Church can understand its own origin and its own goal only as it understands its unity with Israel. Precisely in its Gentile Christian members it must perceive that it would itself be forsaken by God if God had really forsaken Israel."[22] So Barth actually

[20] Karl Barth, *Church Dogmatics*, ed. G. W. Bromiley and T. F. Torrance (Edinburgh: T. & T. Clark, 1957), vol. II, Part 2, The Doctrine of God, 296; hereafter references are in the format CD II/2, 296.
[21] CD II/2, 284.   [22] Ibid.

takes Calvin's point about the irrevocable election of the Jews, yet he will not follow Calvin's way of describing it. He thinks that it is inexcusable Christian anti-Semitism to say that the wrath of God is unleashed against the Jewish people and that the Jewish people themselves are lost so that you only have this hidden remnant of the elect remaining within them.[23] So hope in the revelation of Jesus Christ, which is the life of faith, stands or falls with hope for Israel. However, Barth does not expect the reverse to be the case. The hope of the Jews does not rest with their hope for the Church, nor must the Synagogue see the Church as essential to its own witness.[24]

But then when you ask Barth what it is that Israel attests, what it is that Israel bears witness to and represents, and why its witness is inseparable from that of the Church, then Barth's Israel ends up looking a lot like Calvin's Israel. It is an Israel that rejects grace, an Israel under judgment, an Israel that summons God's wrath upon itself, an Israel that perishes, an Israel that is in some ways being annihilated before our very eyes. "Israel is the people of the Jews which resists its divine election. It is the community of God insofar as this community has to exhibit also the unwillingness, incapacity, and unworthiness of humanity with respect to the love of God directed to him."[25] And they do this especially by delivering up their Messiah to be crucified. The Jews represent, Israel represents, the sin which Christ takes upon himself. In other words, the Jews are elected to bear witness to the human rejection of grace, and the misery of humanity that comes from this rejection, before, during, and after Christ, to this very day. This is what they always attest; this is what they are called and elected to attest. Barth is quite clear about this. He acknowledges that there is faith in Israel every now and then, but that is the exception that proves the rule. "The exception of the few believers in Israel does not cancel the rule according to which Israel as a whole hears and does not believe and is thus disobedient to its election."[26] Indeed, by the time of Jesus, there was no faith left in

[23] Ibid., 290.   [24] Ibid., 200.   [25] Ibid., 198.   [26] Ibid., 239.

Israel. Jesus was the only faithful Israelite left. "Ultimately they seem to disappear completely in the melancholy total aspect of the issue of Israel's history. As genuinely consoled and blessed there remains finally only the one Jesus of Nazareth."[27]

Israel is called and elected in order to bear witness to the sin of humanity that God has taken upon himself in Jesus Christ. Its election cannot reveal anything more than this rejection of grace and the fatal consequences that follow.

> Israel can set forth *only* the sheer stark judgment of God, *only* the obduracy and consequent misery of humanity, *only* the sentence and punishment that God in his mercy has chosen himself to prevent them from falling on us, *only* the realm of darkness as covered and removed and destroyed by the saving fashion of Christ, *only* the existence and nature of fallen man in its futile revolt against God as completely outmoded and superseded in virtue of the mercy of God in Jesus Christ. This is how Israel punishes itself for its sectarian self-assertion. But it cannot alter the fact that even in this way it discharges exactly the service for which it is elected.[28]

Israel is loved by God, and its role is to say No to that love and to suffer all the consequences of that rejection before our eyes, and thereby to show us exactly what it was and is that Christ takes from all of us. This is the hell, if you will, that God chooses for God's self in Christ, and the Jews can do no other than to represent this to us before, during and after the time of Christ. Barth reaffirms this claim in his book *Christ and Adam*, published in 1952. It is amazing to me that someone can write sentences like this in the 1950s, but I think it is important to hear this voice. Barth says, "The Jew who provides the proof of the existence of God," and he thinks they are the only proof for the existence of God that we have:

> provides at the same time the proof of his own sin and his own fall. The Jew is the transgression that abounded. The *only thing* that the

[27] Ibid., 266–67.   [28] Ibid., 208–9, my emphasis.

Jews' history can reveal is human rebellion. The *only thing* that the Jews' destiny can reveal is human misery. The anti-Semitic misunderstanding is natural and quite understandable. But that does not alter the fact that the mission of the Jews is to represent in themselves human rebellion and human suffering, and so to provide in themselves the only genuine and convincing proof that humanity can provide of the existence of God.[29]

The Jews prove that God exists by the suffering that they have to endure for their rebellion. They suffer at the hands of God for their sin. All through their history, they are being destroyed and preserved, and thereby prove that God exists.

In the destiny of this people, in its continual abandonment, extermination, and destruction from its suffering in Egypt to the final fall of Jerusalem and beyond that down to the present day, in the weakness, torment, and sickness of this Job, this strangest of God's servants among the peoples – it has to pay dearly for being among God's chosen people – there is mirrored the radicalism in which God himself makes real his mercy with man, the enigmatic character of God's self-surrender.[30]

There is a paradox at work here, and I think there is something quite elegant that Barth is trying to do in the midst of this rather astonishing language. On the one hand, the Jews are elected to suffer abandonment, extermination, and destruction at the hands of God, from the captivity in Egypt through the final fall of Jerusalem right down to the present day. Barth reaffirms this description of the Jews in 1953. "To be flesh means to exist with the 'children' of Israel under the wrath and judgment of the electing and loving God. To be flesh is to be in a state of perishing before God ... At this point we can and must think of the history of the Jews right up to our own day."[31] On

---

[29] Karl Barth, *Christ and Adam*, trans. T. A. Small (Eugene, OR: Wipf and Stock Publishers, 2004), 57, my emphasis.
[30] CD II/2, 261.   [31] CD IV/1, 174–75.

the other hand, the elect Jews reveal to all of us the sin of which we are also guilty, which God has elected to take upon himself in Christ. "From the negative standpoint that is the mystery of the Jews and their representative existence. That is what anti-Semitism old and new has thundered, but without understanding that we have a mirror held up to the men of all peoples."[32] The suffering and destruction of this people at the hands of God reveals to us who we are, who we Gentiles are. It is the mirror in which we can finally see our true reflection, and therefore anything that we may say against the Jews is really being said against ourselves. In the Jews we also we have the representation of what the eternal Son of God in Christ has willed to take on God's self, and by that he means the divine nature of Christ in particular. The Son of God wills to take the place of sinful Israel that is perishing under the wrath of God, so that the Son of God himself becomes Israel perishing under the wrath and judgment of God. Christ therefore truly accomplishes in himself the divine annihilation of sin and sinners that annihilates sin with all of its consequences. "In His person He has delivered up us sinners and sin itself to destruction."[33] So there is a kind of divine Tai-Chi taking place in which God takes on himself the Jewish rejection of grace in the crucifixion of Jesus, to take this rejection away from the Jews and do away with it once and for all. God could only take Israel's sin from it by allowing its rejection of grace to land fully upon the eternal Son of God, for "it was only by rejecting Christ that Israel could serve the gracious purposes of God. If grace was to abound, if sin and death were to be removed from the world, Christ *had* to be condemned and *had* to die."[34]

Barth's decisive contribution here is to take away once and for all any attempt to use the crucifixion of Jesus against the Jews, as if this event fundamentally undermined their election by God. If Barth is right about what happened in Christ, then one must categorically

---

[32] Ibid., 171–72.   [33] Ibid., 253.
[34] Barth, *Christ and Adam*, 63.

reject Calvin's claim that by crucifying the Son of God the Jews break the covenant and bring on themselves the severity of divine judgment, thereby laying the grounds for their extreme annihilation. As Barth says, "The implication that [Israel] is therefore accursed of God and the proper object of man's hate and scorn is for the same reason completely invalid and utterly unjustified. Nothing else could have happened."[35] Indeed, since God is taking on himself our rejection of grace when the Jews reject Christ and hand him over to be crucified, then anything that is said against the Jews is ultimately being said against the eternal the Son of God, because God has taken the place of sinful Israel.[36] Barth therefore provides us with a Christological firewall against the kind of theological annihilationism regarding the Jews that one finds in Calvin's theology. Christ takes on himself the Jews' rejection of grace, and therefore has removed it decisively from them. The crucifixion of Jesus is also the mirror of our own rejection of grace. All of us sin; all of us reject grace. That is all we do. We never cooperate. We only say No. God takes our rejection of grace on Godself because God knows we will never say Yes on our own. And so the Jews represent to us our own rejection of and incapacity for grace, along with the annihilation that we should all suffer as a consequence of it, yet God has taken all of this on Godself once and for all in Christ.

The problem as I see it is that Barth's description of the Jews simply does not do justice to Jewish existence, because it defines the Jews exclusively in light of their handing Christ over to be crucified. The rejection of Christ makes Israel into a singular vessel of God's wrath and judgment. "Israel in itself and as such is the 'vessel of dishonor.' It is the witness to the divine judgment" and is therefore "a single 'vessel of wrath.'"[37] Its rejection of the Gospel means that "Israel cuts itself off from God's community and goes into the ghetto."[38] These "dwellers in the ghetto" therefore become "the sick

---

[35] Ibid.   [36] CD IV/1, 172.
[37] CD II/2, 224, 226.   [38] Ibid., 214.

and captive and afflicted" people, "the people and the Synagogue of death."[39] As a consequence, as though this were a matter of empirical observation, the Jews "must now live among the nations the pattern of a historical life which has absolutely no future."[40] In contrast to the life of every other people in history, the Jews "can only lead an outcast, despised, dispersed, unreal life among other nations."[41] One need only think of "Jewish obduracy and melancholy, even Jewish caprice and phantasy, even the Jewish cemetery at Prague" to see in the Jews a people "which steps into the void."[42] It is true that in their life the Jews both prove the existence of God and reveal human sinfulness, but they do so "in the spectral form of the Synagogue," so that "the Jews of the ghetto give this demonstration involuntarily, joylessly, and ingloriously, but they do give it."[43] None of this does justice to Jewish existence before Christ, nor does it do justice to Jewish existence after Christ. I do not know a Jew in the world who would recognize him or herself in these descriptions, who would agree with this description of him or herself. If Barth is right over against Calvin – and I am convinced he is – that we must understand the election of Israel as the election of the whole people, in spite of their rejection of Christ, then we should try our best to do justice to the reality of this one elect people of God, and to their own understanding of themselves, so that they can more or less recognize themselves in what we are saying. The language of misery, suffering, death, judgment, wrath, hopelessness, abandonment, extermination, and destruction, even if it is Christologically intercepted at the last minute, simply does not work, for it defines the Jews exclusively in light of the crucifixion of Jesus. "They have nothing to attest to the world but the shadow of the cross of Jesus Christ that falls upon them."[44] If we are to develop Barth's invaluable insights, over against Calvin, that the Jews as a whole are the elect people of God, and are so irreducibly essential to our own

---

[39] Ibid., 264.   [40] Ibid., 263.   [41] CD II/2, 265.
[42] Ibid., 236.   [43] Ibid., 209.   [44] Ibid., 209.

relationship to the love of God that if God gives up on the Jews, God has given up on all of us, then we need to understand the Jews directly in light of God's love for them, and not in light of claims about their rejection of God's love in Christ.

To his great credit, Barth realizes that this is true, and so he attempts to arrive at a description of the Jews in which they are the attestation of a community loved by God, and not only a community suffering under judgment and wrath. The first attempt at such a description occurs in his discussion of Providence, in which the existence of the Jews is a trace of the governance of the world by Jesus Christ the King. According to Barth, owing to their rejection of their Messiah, the history of the Jews as a people was to come to an end in 70 CE, meaning that they should not even exist as a people any more after that date. "In the year 70, in that destruction of Jerusalem which corresponded in so sinister a way to the death of Jesus … Jews as Jews were not meant to have any continued existence."[45] However, the Jews continue to exist right up to the present day, even after "what was apparently the worst disaster in all their history, completely eclipsing all previous disasters," namely the Shoah, so that now the Jews have once again set up a state in Palestine, for the first time since the Diaspora.[46] Thus the Jews continue to exist even though their existence as a people ended decisively in 70 CE, so that their existence is "non-historical: the history of a guest and alien and stranger and exception among the nations, with the eternal Jew, perhaps, as its legendary pattern."[47] The continued existence of the Jews is therefore a "miracle and a riddle" in whose special history we see a trace of the divine world-governance of Jesus Christ. How then can they continue to exist? They exist because their rejection of God's grace, which was to bring the end of the Jews as a people, has been taken upon God by the coming of Christ, thereby fulfilling the covenant with Israel. Because God has decisively identified with sinful Israel in Christ, the Jews must exist with the same necessity

---

[45] CD III/3, 212.   [46] Ibid.   [47] Ibid., 215.

with which God exists, for God's love for Israel has triumphed in Christ in and for Israel.

> It is because the Jews are this people that it is true of them right up to our own day: "He that toucheth you toucheth the apple of my eye" (Zech. 2:8). But no one can touch the apple of his eye. Therefore the Jews can be despised and hated and oppressed and persecuted and even assimilated, but they cannot really be touched; they cannot be exterminated; they cannot be destroyed. They are the only people that necessarily continues to exist, with the same certainty that God is God.[48]

However, the existence of the Jews constantly gives rise to outbreaks of anti-Semitism, leading the other peoples to seek to persecute, and even eradicate, the Jews in their midst. Barth claims that this anti-Semitism has two sources. One is already quite familiar: the Jews are a mirror to all of us of our rejection of God's grace. "In the Jew there is revealed the primal revolt, the unbelief, the disobedience, in which we are all engaged. In this sense the Jew is the most human of all men. And that is why he is not pleasing to us. That is why we want to remove this alien element from our midst."[49] However, God continues to uphold and protect the Jews in spite of all attempts to remove them from history, which means that at the root of Jewish existence must lie the love of God itself, indeed the election of God itself. And here Barth begins to understand the Jews directly from the perspective of the love of God for them as a people, and not in light of the crucifixion of Jesus. The continued existence of the Jews, even after 70 CE, reveals to all nations and peoples that the Jews alone are the one elect people of God.

> Is it really possible to exist as the Jews have existed? Well, this is what they have done, and in doing it they are obviously a mirror, a mirror of the election of the divine grace and mercy on whose basis they

---

[48] Ibid., 218.   [49] CD III/3, 222.

were clearly able to do it. And not on any other basis! – that is what annoys and irritates us so much from this standpoint.[50]

The existence of the Jews reveals far more than human sin in this portrayal, for their existence also reveals both the sheer gratuity and the offensive particularism of divine election. *Only* the Jews, and no other people, are the beloved people of God; *only* the Jews are the elect people of God. "For in the existence of the Jew we stumble upon the fact that the divine election is a particular election, that we ourselves have been completely overlooked in the particularity of this divine election."[51] The particularity of the election of the Jews offends us Gentile Christians, which explains why we "ransack Christianity for proofs that it is no longer so."[52] For we know that the election of the Jews, enduring to our day long after the events of the death of Jesus and the destruction of Jerusalem, and even after the horrors of the Shoah, means that "to be elect ourselves, for good or evil we must either be Jews or belong to this Jew. And yet who among us is really willing either to learn this or to admit this?"[53]

Barth returns to this aspect of the existence of the Jews – as attesting the divine love and their own gracious election – in his discussion of the mission of the Church toward the end of the *Dogmatics*. Once again he describes the Jews as the one elect people of God, to whom we must be joined if we also are to be elected by God. "They are the people of God loved by him in free grace, elected and called to His service, and originally sent into the world as his witnesses."[54] Unlike his previous position, in which the rebellion of Israel against the grace of God proves the existence of God, Barth now claims that it is the Jews as specially loved and preserved by God throughout their history that demonstrates the existence of God. "It is the Jew, even the unbelieving Jew, so miraculously preserved," not annihilated or exterminated, but preserved, "as we

---

[50] Ibid., 224.   [51] Ibid., 225.   [52] Ibid.
[53] Ibid.   [54] CD IV/3.2, 877.

must say through the many calamities of his history," not divine punishments, but calamities "who as such is the natural historical monument to the love and faithfulness of God," not to the wrath and judgment of God, but to the love and faithfulness of God, "who in concrete form is the epitome of the human freely chosen and blessed by God," not rejected and cursed by God, "who as a living commentary on the Old Testament is the only convincing proof of God outside the Bible."[55] That, I think, is an astonishing statement, and what I want to do in the next chapter is to follow up on this suggestion by Barth, using elements from Calvin's theology, in order to construct a Christian description of the Jewish community which as such is a living monument to the love and faithfulness of God, apart from any consideration of their acceptance or rejection of Jesus Christ.

However, even at this point in his career, Barth is still conflicted regarding his view of the Jews, for in the very same paragraph he claims yet again that the Jews are a people devoid of a future and of blessing. "The Synagogue was and is the organization of a group of men which hastens toward a future that is empty now that He has come who should come, that is still without consolation, which clings to a Word of God that is still unfulfilled."[56] Once again, the Jews are defined and portrayed in light of their rejection of Christ, not in light of their being loved and elected by God. "Necessarily, therefore, the Jew who is uniquely blessed offers the picture of an existence which, *characterized by the rejection of its Messiah* and therefore of its salvation and mission, is dreadfully empty of grace and blessing."[57] Nonetheless, it is most significant that Barth moves from portraying the Jews only as a mirror of human sinfulness and as the vessel of divine judgment and wrath, to seeing them as a mirror of grace and election and as a living natural monument to the love and faithfulness of God. If this is the case, how can they be without a future, without consolation, without grace, without blessing, even given their refusal to believe in Christ?

[55] Ibid.   [56] Ibid.   [57] Ibid., my emphasis.

Barth also laments, apparently for the first time in his *Dogmatics*, the Church's role in relation to the Jews. He insists that the Jews were never to be the object of Christian mission because the Gentile Christians get everything from the Jews. They get God from the Jews, they get the Covenant from the Jews, they get election from the Jews, they get God's presence from the Jews, they get Scripture from the Jews, they get everything from the Jews. "The God whose Word and work it has to attest to the world was the God of Israel before the community itself ever came forth from this people, and to this day He can only be the God of Israel."[58] Gentile Christians do not have anything to give to the Jews, so there can be no mission to the Jews. There is, however, one thing which Gentile Christians owe to the Jews, and that is convincing witness that the God of Israel is savingly, eschatologically present in Jesus Christ, in such a way as to make the Jews jealous of that presence. "It must make dear and desirable and illuminating to it Him whom it has rejected."[59] The Christians owe it to the Jews to give such a compelling testimony to Christ by their life before the Jews, that the Jews would say, "That must be it! Everything we want in the law is even more superlatively found in Christ. I would consider the law to be trash, as Paul says, for the sake of what I now see to be in Christ." Yet Barth acknowledges that for 2,000 years the Church has catastrophically failed to give the Jews such testimony. "In this sense the Church as a whole has made no convincing impression on the Jew as a whole. It has debated with him, tolerated him, persecuted him, or abandoned him to persecution without protest. What is worse, it has made baptism an entrance card into the best European society."[60] But the one thing it owed to the Jews, which is compelling and convincing testimony that the God of Israel is fully present in a transformative way in Jesus Christ, it has failed to offer.

Thus it still owes everything to those to whom it is indebted for everything. This failure, which is often unconscious, or perhaps

---

[58] Ibid.   [59] Ibid., 878.   [60] Ibid.

concealed by all kinds of justifiable or unjustifiable countercharges against the Jews, is one of the darkest chapters in the whole history of Christianity and one of the most serious of all wounds in the body of Christ.[61]

In fact, he goes on to say that there is no division in the body of Christ that comes close to the seriousness of this division. I personally think that this acknowledgement is astonishing, and I will leave that as the last contribution of Barth to this discussion.

So we can see both Calvin and Barth wrestling very powerfully with this issue. Given the rejection of Christ and the Gospel by the Jews, has God in fact abandoned the Jews? Or is Jesus in fact not the Christ promised to the Jews? Are the promises to Abraham totally false, or is Jesus in fact not the one who was promised to the Jews? This is an incredibly difficult question. It cuts to the very heart of the Gospel. There is nothing that threatens the Gospel as much as this question: secularism, modernity, and skepticism do not threaten the Gospel at all by comparison, for it calls into question the very unity of the Bible. So it is not surprising that Calvin and Barth wrestle so vigorously and in some ways so conflictedly over this question. But I think that Barth is right at the end of the day, when he insists that the Jewish community is the one elect people of God: they always were and they always will be. God only loves us if we are loved in fellowship with that one beloved community. So the Jews, for Christians, are irreplaceable, and are absolutely essential, in a way that Christians are not for Jews. The Jews are the one elect people of God, and no one is elected and loved who is not loved in relation to Israel. "What the history of the Jews tells us is that the divine election is the election of another. Our election can only be in and with this other."[62] At his best, Calvin knows this to be true: the covenant with Abraham is the foundation for the adoption of the Gentiles, and stands even when the Gentiles are included by

---

[61] Ibid.   [62] CD III/3, 225.

means of the Gospel. "When the doctrine of the Gospel was manifested and shone forth, it did not remove the Jews from the covenant which God had long before made with them. On the contrary, it has rather joined us to them." Thus "it nevertheless remains true, that we are not accounted among the children of God unless we have been grafted into the stock of Abraham."[63] I think Barth is also right over and against Calvin, that it is not enough to have a hidden remnant of the elect in the midst of the unbelieving, reprobate community of the Jews; the whole people are elect, even in the midst of their refusal to believe in Christ. Finally, I think that Barth is also correct when he claims that the election of the Jews is manifested not in the death, but in the life of the Jewish community. If you know the Jewish community, it is anything but dead. It is alive, so much so that it makes Gentile Christians look like we are sound asleep. It is vigorous, living, argumentative, active, intelligent, and sparkly. Even secular Jews are that way, it's incredible! That is what I miss most at Notre Dame; there are not enough Jews, and far too many Gentile Christians! So the Jews as such are a living monument to the love of God, are a mirror of the grace and faithfulness of God, are a living testimony to the election of God.

But then how do we make sense out of this description? How do we make sense out of the fact that the blessing of God still abides in Israel even when Israel says No to Jesus? How can God bless those who will never, ever believe the Gospel? I remember John Cavadini telling us at the University memorial service for Rabbi Signer, that Michael sat down in his office one day and said, "John, let me just put it to you straight. I never have, I do not now, and I never will believe that your Jesus is our Messiah." So that is the situation. The people that will only say No are still blessed by God. The people that say No still live in the presence of God. The people that say No to Christ are still objects of divine faithfulness. How do we make sense out of this? Can we make sense out of this in a way that is fair

---

[63] Comm. Psalm 47:9, CO 31:471A; CTS 9:169.

to the way Jews understand themselves, and that is still faithful to the witness of the Scriptures? Can we do this without undermining what Christians want to say about Jesus Christ, while also honoring what the Jews want to say about their relationship with God? I want to explore that issue in the next chapter, following leads left by Calvin and Barth, though the position I will advance is not found in either theologian.

4 | The restoration of Israel by gospel and law: Calvin and Ezra the Scribe

This chapter will attempt to explore an answer to the questions posed in the previous chapter by appealing directly to Calvin and the Bible, to see if we might be able to develop a positive theological understanding of Israel and the Jews based on these sources. I will set forth a trajectory in Calvin that I hope will allow us better to understand the covenant made with Israel on its own terms, without mediating this covenant through Christ, so that Christians can acknowledge the integrity of this covenant on its own terms, based on our own Scriptures. As we have seen in the previous chapter, the impressive attempts made by Calvin and Barth to unite the covenant with Israel with the work of God in Christ wind up succumbing to oppositional forms of thinking. No matter how positively Israel is understood, it is inevitably brought under the shadow of the cross, and is understood in terms of the categories of human sin and divine wrath. Is there a way of understanding the history of this covenant that is less toxic, less oppositional, less vengeful, if you will? You can tell that Calvin and Barth have a hard time restraining themselves. They will say positive things about the Jews after the death of Christ, but then they will appeal to the Jewish refusal to believe in Christ and the Gospel, and see the Jews as under judgment, under wrath, with no blessing, with no hope for the future. If you look at the history of Christianity from the very early days until now, this is the tendency one sees, a combination of grudging generosity followed by incredible vituperation. Is there a way out of this dynamic that allows us to see God's relationship to the Jews on its own terms, without appealing to Christ and the Gospel, but based on the Scriptures that Christians claim as their own? Can we come to an understanding of the blessing of God in the Jewish community in terms that Christians can recognize as fully consistent with their Scriptures, and which Jews can recognize as consistent with their own self-understanding?

I would like to begin with two quotes from Calvin and Barth that represent their best efforts to understand God's relationship with the Jews on its own terms, though subsequently we will be working mainly from Calvin and the Scriptures. In his discussion of the relationship of circumcision to infant baptism, Calvin notes how the promise of God associated with circumcision is still in effect, so that the blessing of God is still to be found in the community of the circumcised in his own day.

> Yet, despite the great obstinacy with which they continue to wage war against the gospel, we must not despise them, while we consider that, for the sake of the promise, God's blessing still rests with them. For the apostle indeed testifies that it will never be completely taken away: "For the gifts and the calling of God are without repentance" [Rom. 11:29, Vg.].[1]

Can we understand how the blessing of God remains with the Jewish community on its own terms, without attempting to withdraw it again based on the refusal of this community to believe in Christ? Barth also attempts to give a portrayal of the Jews that places them directly in relation to the love, faithfulness and blessing of God. "It is the Jew, even the unbelieving Jew, so miraculously preserved as we must say, through the many calamities of his history, who as such is the natural historical monument to the love and faithfulness of God, who in concrete form is the epitome of the person freely chosen and blessed by God."[2] Can we develop this insight in a way that avoids Barth's subsequent claim to take the love and blessing of God away from the Jews, leaving them without hope for the future? What is

---

[1] Inst. IV.xvi.14, OS V.317–18; LCC 1337.   [2] CD IV/3.2, 877.

significant in both of these passages is that they refer directly to God. They do not place the Jews in relation to Christ, they place them in relation to God. In what follows I want to develop what kind of difference it would make if we switched the terms of this discussion from Christ to God, in spite of the discomfort this might cause those deeply committed to the doctrine of the Trinity in all matters theological. My precedent for making this move is found in Calvin's theology itself, which may be one reason why his understanding of the Trinity could never put his interlocutors completely at ease. As we have seen, Calvin thought very deeply about the meaning and scope of the history of Israel, from the calling of Abram to the destruction of the Second Temple, in a way that makes him virtually unique in the history of the Christian tradition. I can think of no other theologian who dedicated as much attention as Calvin did to thinking through the meaning of every aspect of Israel's life, not only as recorded in Scripture, but also in extra canonical sources such as First and Second Maccabees and Josephus. Yet it is clear that Calvin has two distinct ways of understanding that history. The first, which we discussed in the previous chapter, is through the symbols of the coming Christ given to Israel from Adam to John the Baptist. There is an abundance of symbols that Calvin sees in Israel's life which represent Christ to them in an anticipatory way, but which also offer the grace of Christ to them as truly as this grace is offered to the Christian community. However, as we have seen, when you track Israel's history on those terms, you are on a collision course, culminating in the crucifixion of Jesus and the rejection of the Gospel for the sake of the Law of Moses. Sacrifices in particular offer the forgiveness of sin won once and for all on the cross of Christ to the Israelites and Jews, but when Christ actually dies, the Jews allegedly break their covenant with God and are rejected as God's people. So understanding the history of Israel as a symbolic representation of the reality of Christ does not get us out of oppositional thinking, and inevitably winds up seeing the Jews negatively as those who reject Christ. That is also the problem with Barth's way of understanding this history. Since Christ is the center of all human history, the shadow of the cross will inevitably fall over Israel's history.

But Calvin also speaks of God's relationship to the Israelites in terms of symbols of the presence of God, from the patriarchs and matriarchs right up to the destruction of the Temple in 70 CE. In other words, Israel is not just related to God by means of its relationship to the coming of Christ, but is also related directly to God all along through the presence of God in its midst, which is represented to the Israelites in visible and tangible ways throughout their history. The symbols of God's presence have a vertical reference to God, and not a horizontal reference to Christ. The symbols of the Church have the same vertical referent. Calvin will always point out the way that the face of God shown to the Israelites and Jews in the Ark of the Covenant is like the face of God revealed to the Church in the Word and sacraments. He is not led to contrast the symbols of God's presence before and after the coming of Christ, as he always does with regard to the symbols of Christ, especially the sacrifices. He rather seeks always to see the parallels between the symbols of God's presence in Israel and those in the Church, and will even draw comfort for the Church of his day from the symbols of God's presence in Israel. If the positive meaning of these symbols may be seen in the Christian community which no longer follows the Law, would it not be possible for Christians to see a positive meaning in these symbols in the community that continues to observe the Law, the one elect people of God?

So what do we learn from Calvin if we look at the history of Israel and the Jews via the presence of God in their life? Are there aspects of this history that we can draw out more fully beyond the time of Christ, in ways that go beyond Calvin? Calvin is particularly helpful in this regard, for his attention to the symbols of divine presence alerts him to the decisive moment in all of Israel's history, namely the exile to Babylon and the restoration after the exile. Calvin claims that the beginning of the kingdom of Jesus Christ is to be found in the return of the Jews from Babylon, so this moment is of decisive importance to him. As we shall see, Calvin attends in great detail to the rebuilding of the Temple, but he entirely neglects another aspect of the restored community, and that is the presence of Ezra the Scribe and the pivotal role that he plays in the restored community. Calvin's neglect of Ezra is not surprising, given that most Christians have never even heard his name, but in Rabbinic literature, Ezra is second in importance only to Moses. In some ways he is more import-ant than Moses, for without him the Law of Moses would not be taught in the Jewish community after Babylon. So Ezra is absolutely pivotal in the restoration of the Jewish community after Babylon, for in a way he is Moses to the generation that returns. The Sages in the Rabbinic schools draw a direct line from Ezra through the very confusing, turbulent, often perplexing Second Temple Period to themselves, and credit him with instituting the Great Assembly (which may appear in the New Testament as the Sanhedrin), which establishes the continuity of the teaching of the Law from Ezra to the Sages. So Ezra is a pivotal figure for the Jews, and should be for Calvin, for he is found in the same narrative that sets forth the res-toration of the Temple and the city of Jerusalem in which Calvin was so intensely interested. Can Ezra help us to see how God is pre-sent to the Jews after the return from Babylon, and why the Jews are adamant that the presence of God is essentially tied to the teaching and observance of the Law of Moses?

In order to explore this issue, we need first to turn to Calvin's discussion of the symbols of God's presence in Israel. Even though God is present to Abraham and Sarah, Calvin sees this theme really starting to emerge in the Exodus, for it is during this time that the presence of God is disclosed to the Israelites, as much in divine sym-bols as in God's actions. Indeed, God will reveal that God is truly present in the symbol of God's presence by acting in association with the symbol. For Calvin, the Exodus is the action of God that is the archetype of the grace and presence of God, so that every sub-sequent act of God is a confirmation of this exemplary act. On the one hand, the Exodus acts retroactively by confirming the adoption of the people of Abraham by their liberation from Egypt. On the other hand, the Exodus acts prospectively as a pledge of the way God will continue to act toward Israel in the future. "The deliverance from Egypt, having been the chief and lasting pledge of the divine favor, which practically ratified their adoption under the patriarch, is briefly adverted to by the author. He would intimate that in that remarkable exodus, proof had been given to all succeeding ages of the love which God entertained for God's people."[3] The Exodus is therefore a pledge of divine love which both confirms their adoption retroactively, and which promises God's love to the people from that time forward, without any end in sight.

So the Exodus itself reveals to the Israelites, and to Calvin, the essential character of God. One of the central principles of Calvin's theology is that God is always like God. God may act differently at times, but God will always act the same way toward God's people. So the pledge of love given to the Israelites in the Exodus is for perpetuity. This is why Daniel can still appeal to the Exodus when he is in exile in Babylon. "For when God led his people out of Egypt, he did not set before them any momentary benefit merely, but he bore witness to the adoption of Abraham on the condition of his being their perpetual Savior."[4] The Exodus therefore pledges God to be the redeemer of the children of Abraham from that day forward. Calvin gives a rather elegant interpretation of the Passover ceremony that highlights this aspect of the Exodus.

> In effect, then, the celebration of the Passover taught the Israelites that it was not lawful to have regard to any other God beside their Redeemer; and also that it was right and just for them to consecrate themselves to God's service, since God had restored them from death to life; and thus, as in a glass or picture, he represented to their eyes his grace; and desired that they should on every succeeding year

---

[3] Comm. Psalm 68:8, CO 31:622; CTS 10:12.
[4] Comm. Daniel 9:15–17, CO 41:153; CTS 25:175.

recognize what they had formerly experienced, lest it should ever depart from their memory.[5]

So the Passover reminds the children of Abraham of their deliverance from Egypt, so that they might see God's gracious presence in their midst today, and be assured that God will act in the same way toward them in the future. As we shall see, Calvin will see decisive confirmation of this pledge in the return of the Jews from Babylon.

Moreover, Calvin links this symbol of God's gracious presence in the Exodus, commemorated in the Passover, with the symbols of God's presence during the wilderness journey, especially the cloud by day and the fire by night. He claims that these symbols are given as a perpetual proof of God's love for God's people, so that even when they are no longer visible, God is nonetheless still present with God's people. "This continued display of God's goodness and presence was surely an unquestionable proof of God's perpetual love, an open demonstration that God had adopted the children of Abraham to foster them under God's protection even to the end."[6] Note that Calvin does not draw any kind of temporal limit to this pledge of love for the children of Abraham. It is without end. And so when the prophet appeals to this visible symbol of God's presence from an earlier age even when it is no longer present in his day, Calvin says he is doing so to show that the presence of God symbolized by the fire and the cloud is still present among the people now even though they no longer have these signs. Once a pledge of God's presence is given, the reality it symbolizes is never taken away. "God meant to testify in all ages that God's presence was ever with God's people, according as he employed temporal signs, not only for their benefit to whom they were exhibited, but also for the benefit of those who were to succeed them ... And as God had appeared openly in the desert to their fathers, so their posterity might well be assured

---

[5] Comm. Exodus 12:1, CO 24:285–86; CTS 3:456.
[6] Comm. Psalm 105:39, CO 32:113; CTS 11:202.

that he would also be near to them," even though they no longer see these symbols.[7] Calvin also sees the land of Canaan as a very concrete, real, and serious pledge of God's favor, adoption and goodness towards the people, and thus of God's presence with them. "The land was a symbol or an earnest and a pledge of God's paternal favor," promising to the people that God will always be their God.[8]

Most significantly for Calvin, during the wilderness journey God institutes a perpetual symbol of God's presence among the people, namely the Tabernacle and everything associated with it, especially the Ark of the Covenant. And of course the irony in the narrative of Exodus is that as God is revealing this symbol of God's presence to Moses for the sake of the people, they are busy building one of their own down below. This reveals to Calvin the perpetual conflict between the symbols of God's presence that God institutes for us, and those that we create on our own, which is one of his central concerns in his criticism of humanly devised images in worship. The concern, therefore, is essential to the faithful: How do we know that God is present among us? God addresses this concern by instituting symbols of God's presence – the Tabernacle and the Ark – that can travel with the people and thus be perpetual symbols that God is with them. Calvin was especially interested in the Ark of the Covenant, for this is the superlative symbol of God's presence among the children of Abraham. "Besides many signs of his presence, he formerly exhibited a singular proof of it in the ark, from which he both gave answers and heard his people, in order to put forth his power in helping them. For this reason it was termed 'the Glory of God.'"[9] In particular, the tablets of the Law give the Ark this centrality, for the Law of Moses itself is a confirmation of the covenant made with Abraham, thereby confirming the adoption of his children by God.

[7] Comm. Psalm 99:6, CO 32:53; CTS 11:80–81.
[8] Comm. Jeremiah 11:1–5, CO 38:102; CTS 18:77.
[9] Comm. Romans 9:4, CO 49:172; CNTC 8:194.

He had indeed made with Abraham an eternal and inviolable covenant; but because it had grown into disregard from the lapse of time, and the carelessness of mankind, it became needful that it should again be renewed. To this end, then, it was engraved upon the tablets of stone, and written in a book, that the marvelous grace, which God had conferred upon the race of Abraham, should never sink into oblivion.[10]

One of my Jewish friends in Jerusalem is amazed by this part of Calvin, because unlike Luther, Calvin loves Moses, and sees the giving of the Law at Sinai as an act of grace, confirming the adoption of the children of Abraham. This insight could also have helped Calvin to see how decisive the Law will be in association with the presence of God with the people after Babylon, which unfortunately he does not see as clearly. In any case, Calvin thinks that the placement of the tablets of the covenant of the law in the Ark of the Covenant is what makes it the most important monument to God's grace. Moses was sent by God to confirm God's grace by the giving of the law, and so the tables of the law symbolize in a very real way for Calvin the gracious presence of God among the people of Abraham. And that is why the commandments are engraved on tablets of stone. This really is an astonishing claim for Calvin to make, as you would never find Martin Luther saying that Moses was sent to confirm the grace of God for the people. Calvin's insight here into the essential relationship of the presence of God with the Law of Moses will also allow us to see the same connection when we get to Ezra, in a way Calvin himself neglected to see.

Since the Ark contains the tablets of the Law, the Ark will become the focal point of God's dwelling among the people from Sinai onward. Calvin says that the Ark bears testimony to the presence of God in a way that met the needs of the faithful, to remind them of God's present goodness so that they might not think that they sought

---

[10] Comm. Exodus 19:1, CO 24:192; CTS 3:313.

God in vain.[11] The Israelites rightly thought that God was present among them in the Tabernacle and in the Ark, so that when they directed their prayers to the Tabernacle, they were directing their prayers to God. Calvin of course does not want the pious to focus on the presence of God in the symbol to such a degree that they come to think that God is contained in the symbol. Rather, they are to ascend from the symbol to God. But note that they can ascend directly to God, and do not have to look forward to the coming Christ who has not yet appeared. The symbol brings them into relationship with God, and so as long as they ascend from the symbol to the God who is present in that symbol, they are using the symbol of God's presence rightly. Calvin is thinking especially of Solomon's magnificent prayer of dedication in the Temple. Solomon asks God, "But will God indeed dwell on the earth? Even heaven and the highest heaven cannot contain you, much less this house that I have built!" (1 Kings 8:27). However, Solomon takes confidence from the promise of God to dwell in the Temple. "Hear the plea of your servant and of your people Israel when they pray toward this place; O hear in heaven your dwelling place; heed and forgive" (1 Kings 8:30). Calvin always has this association, which I think actually really works in this context, of God coming down to meet us in the symbols of God's presence that we see, to lift us up to God's presence which we do not see. So God becomes visible and descends so that we might ascend to the invisible. But the visible presence of God is real, and is not an illusion or something fabricated on the basis of our faith. Calvin adamantly defends the true presence of God in the Ark of Testimony, in the Tabernacle. "As the sanctuary was the pledge or token of the covenant of God, David beheld the presence of God's promised grace there, as if it had been represented in a mirror."[12] David can see God's grace in the Tabernacle, in the place of worship, as though it had become visible.

[11] Comm. Psalm 26:8, CO 31:268–69; CTS 8:446–47.
[12] Comm. Psalm 28:2, CO 31:281; CTS 8:466–67.

Even though the Ark is the primary symbol of the presence of God, Calvin also includes within the visibility of God the entire worship life instituted by the Law of Moses. All of the ceremonies, prayers, and sacrifices set before the Israelites the presence of God.

> David does not simply speak of the presence of God, but of the presence of God in connection with certain symbols; for he sets before himself the Tabernacle, the altar, the sacrifices, and other ceremonies by which God had testified that he would be near his people; and that it behooved the faithful in seeking to approach God, to begin by those things.

Calvin goes on to draw a parallel to his own day, for the symbols and ceremonies of the Gospel testify to the presence of God today just as the ceremonies and symbols of the Law did for the Israelites. "Accordingly, when we see the marks of the divine presence, engraven on the word or on external symbols, we can say with David that there is the face of God."[13] So the same face of God that appeared to the Israelites in their ceremonies and symbols is appearing in the symbols and worship of Calvin's church. I think that is significant. In other words you see an analogical application of this phenomenon rather than a kind of collision between the two. I am not saying Calvin is going to say what I want to say, but I think there is a door opening here that leads us in a more promising direction. So the Ark in particular, but also all of the worship surrounding the Ark, is a pledge of God's presence, and Calvin is very willing to make the application to his own day in terms of the manifestation of God's presence in the Church.

> What is the design of the preaching of the word, the sacraments, the holy assemblies, and the whole external government of the church, but that we may be united to God? It is not, therefore, without good reason that David extols so highly the service of God appointed in

---

[13] Comm. Psalm 42:2, CO 31:426–27; CTS 9:130.

the law, seeing God exhibited himself to his saints in the ark of the covenant, and thereby gave them a certain pledge of speedy succor whenever they should invoke him for aid.[14]

It is quite remarkable how seamlessly Calvin moves from the purpose of the worship instituted by the Gospel to the purpose of the worship under the Law, for what happens in both of them is that the faithful are united to God. He does not speak about union with Christ, nor does he mention Christ as mediating our union with God. So this is the opening in Calvin that I would like to pursue more fully.

The symbols of divine presence that begin in the Exodus and the Tabernacle ultimately culminate for Calvin in the Temple in Jerusalem. Calvin's attention to these symbols of divine presence lead him to realize the absolutely central role that Jerusalem plays in understanding the presence of God in Israel, for the Temple in Jerusalem is the focal point of the presence of God in Israel. He insists that God's promise to dwell in the Temple forever is not an empty promise.

> The amount of what is stated is, that whenever the people should call upon God in the Temple, it would manifestly appear, from the effect which would follow, that the Ark of the Covenant was not a vain and illusory symbol of the presence of God, because God would always stretch forth his omnipotent arm for the sure defense and protection of his people.[15]

Even the palaces in Jerusalem and the walls of Jerusalem and the mountains surrounding Jerusalem become symbols of God's very real presence among the people. "God would have them to behold, as it were, the marks of his grace wherever they turned themselves, or rather, to recognize him as present in these marks."[16] The marks of

---

[14] Comm. Psalm 24:7, CO 31:248; CTS 8:409.
[15] Comm. Psalm 24:8, CO 31:249; CTS 8:412.
[16] Comm. Psalm 48:14, CO 31:480; CTS 9:232.

God's grace were so concretely present in Jerusalem that the enemies of Israel would flee simply upon seeing the city with its palaces and Temple (Psalm 48).

Calvin's appreciation for the symbols of God's presence in Jerusalem means that he is quite sensitive to the devastating effect the Babylonian invasion and exile will have on the Israelites. The destruction of the Temple, the destruction of the palaces, the destruction of the walls, the destruction of Jerusalem, and the exile of the people from the land which was itself a pledge of God's grace, quite rightly forms for Calvin the most profound crisis in the history of Israel. This event breaks the historical narrative and brings it to a kind of frightening pause, making it the axial moment of the Scriptural narrative. Indeed, the whole Bible could be seen as being written to understand how Israel was taken into exile in Babylon, and what the Jews should do once they return. Calvin sees this crisis very clearly. This is why for him the kingdom of Christ begins with the return of the Jews from Babylon. "For it ought to be considered one and the same favor of God, that is, that he brought back his people from exile, that they might at length enjoy quiet and solid happiness when the kingdom of David should again be established."[17] Calvin is therefore intensely interested in what happens in Babylon, and how the community is restored once they return, for he knows that the exile of the people disrupts and apparently undermines every symbol of God's presence, in a way that must have been absolutely terrifying. Calvin knows that it must have seemed to all appearances that the covenant with the children of Abraham had come to an end. The land is a pledge of God's adoption; they are exiled from the land. The Temple is a symbol of God's presence; it is destroyed, and Ezekiel even sees God standing at the threshold of the Temple before God departs (Ezekiel 10:18–19). The city is a symbol of God's presence: it is burnt to the ground. The kings and priests are signs of God's presence; they are all taken into exile. The sacrifices, the priesthood, and

---

[17] Comm. Jeremiah 33:17–18, CO 39:71; CTS 20:260.

the whole worship of God come to an end. It looks as though every single promise God has ever made is null and void. Thus, when the prophet cries out, "Alas! O Lord God, will you destroy the remnant of Israel by pouring forth your anger?" (Ezekiel 9:8), Calvin notes that God seems to have abandoned Jerusalem, and hence to have departed from God's people.

> For that city remained a testimony of God's covenant, and as yet some safety could be hoped for as long as it was around, but although after it was cut off, the faithful wrestled with that temptation, yet the contest was hard and fatiguing, for no one thought that any memorial of God's covenant could flourish when that city was extinct.[18]

So with the disappearing of the symbols of the presence of God, what becomes of the presence of God? This becomes for Calvin the central concern for the community during this time.

Interestingly, Calvin thinks that God's promise to dwell in the Temple forever means that the Temple in a sense still stands because of the promise even after it is destroyed by the Babylonians. The promise to which Calvin returns over and over again is found in Psalm 132:13–14, "For the Lord has chosen Zion. The Lord has desired it for his habitation. 'This is my resting-place forever. Here I will dwell for I have desired it.'" So the Temple stands because of this promise even after it has been burnt to the ground by the Babylonians. This is why Daniel turns to destroyed Jerusalem to pray when he is in Babylon, for God is still present there because of the promise even though the Temple can no longer be seen. "But he so departed, that the place still remained sacred, and the temple stood before God though it had been overthrown in the eyes of men. The visible appearance of the temple was taken away, but meanwhile, since the temple was founded on the promise of God, it stood among its ruins."[19] This is why Haggai could prophesy that

[18] Comm. Ezekiel 9:8, CO 40:203; CTS 22:314.
[19] Comm. Ezekiel 10:19, CO 40:222–23; CTS 22:342.

the second Temple would be more glorious than the first, and Isaiah could describe the glory of the second Temple. The temple exists in the promise, and therefore it will most certainly be rebuilt. "Since therefore the Temple stood before God," even though it was not visibly standing anymore, "because it was founded on his promise, this temporary desertion could not abolish what I have said concerning God's perpetual station."[20] So the presence of God never really left Jerusalem because God promised to be there forever.

Moreover, when God departed the Temple, God did so to go into exile with the captives, to be present to God's people there. This is quite noteworthy, as the Rabbis say something quite similar about the divine presence in exile. When Ezekiel describes God as being a sanctuary to the exiles (Ezek. 11:16), Calvin notes the way the Babylonians had total contempt for the Jews because they had destroyed their glorious Temple, and thought that this proved that God was no longer present with them. They thought, "Where is your God? We have destroyed the symbol of God's presence." The prophet therefore assures the people that God dwelt with them and was really present with them in their exile, forming their sanctuary to protect them from their enemies. Even as God had been present with Abraham in his exile in Canaan, before the Tabernacle was given, so God would be present with the children of Abraham in Babylon, even after the Temple had been destroyed. "So also in this place God says by a figure that God was their sanctuary, not that he had erected an altar there, but because the Israelites were destitute of any external pledge and symbol, he reminds them that the thing itself was not entirely taken away, since God has his wings outstretched to cherish and defend them."[21] So the Temple stands because God promised to dwell there forever, and the presence of God departs from the Temple to go with the people into exile, to care for them there until they would be restored to the land.

---

[20] Comm. Ezekiel 10:19, CO 40:222–23; CTS 22:342.
[21] Comm. Ezekiel 11:14–16, CO 20:240; CTS 22:367–68.

By focusing on the presence of God among the people, Calvin highlights the importance both of the restoration of the people to the land and the restoration of the Temple. This is the turning point of the whole Scriptural narrative for Calvin. He understands why the prophets say that the return of the people from Babylon is a remarkable demonstration of God's grace, confirming the grace of the Exodus and in some sense eclipsing that event. The symbol of God's love and presence in the Exodus is confirmed by what God does in bringing the people back from Babylon. "It amounts to this, that when God shall bring back the Church from the captivity in Babylon, the deliverance will be of a kind not less striking and magnificent than when, at an early period, the nation went out of Egypt."[22] And as the Exodus also revealed to the Israelites how God would act toward them in the future, so the return from exile is a pledge of God's gracious presence that extends all the way to Calvin's day. "From this example we ought to consider how God will be to us, so as to draw this conclusion, that in the future God will always be like himself."[23] Just as the Exodus reveals to us the character of God, so the return from exile confirms that character, so that we can know how God will act toward us today. Again, we see that the discussion of the gracious presence of God leads Calvin to seek continuity between Israel's history and the present, which appears not to be disrupted by the death and resurrection of Christ.

Since the Temple was founded on the eternal promise of God, and stood on this promise even when it had been destroyed, Calvin sees the restoration of the Temple, and the return of the presence of God to the Temple, as essential to the restoration of the people after their exile.

> It was eventually seen in a very striking manner that this promise, that "this is my rest forever," was the promise of an infallible God, when after the Temple had been overthrown, the altar cast

[22] Comm. Isaiah 4:5, CO 36:99; CTS 13:157.
[23] Comm. Isaiah 51:9, CO 37:232–33; CTS 16:76.

down, and the whole frame of the legal service interrupted, the glory of the Lord afterward returned to it once more and remained there up to the advent of Christ.

God remained true to God's promise to dwell in the Temple forever, and to hear the prayers of God's people from there. The people could only be restored, then, when this symbol of God's presence was truly restored. When the prophet says, "And I will glorify the house of my glory," Calvin says:

> Under the glorification of the Temple, he declares the true restoration of the people, for the chief part of their happiness was that the Temple should stand in which people called on God in a right manner, and we must begin with this, that God reigns among us by which we are made truly happy. For this reason, when the Lord declares that the Church shall be restored, he mentions the Temple, the glory of which he will restore.[24]

So the glory of the Temple is essential to the restoration of the people, for the people are only restored when God dwells in their midst. It is absolutely essential to Calvin that God continues to show signs of God's presence in the second Temple period right through the advent of Christ. Calvin is virtually unique among Christian theologians for the interest he takes in the second Temple period, for it constitutes for him the beginning of the restoration brought about by Jesus Christ, in contrast to Luther, who disparages this period as being nothing but "Judaism."

When we come to the time of Jesus, many of the signs of God's presence have disappeared, especially the gift of prophecy. Calvin thinks that while prophecy may have ceased, so that there did not seem to be any sign of God's presence at this time, God nonetheless showed that God was still present in the Temple by healing in the pool outside of the Temple. This revealed to the Jews that God still

---

[24] Comm. Isaiah 60:7, CO 37:359B; CTS 16:283.

heard their prayers and approved of their worship according to the rites of the law.

> The Lord retained among the Jews this gift of healing that they might know that there was good reason why God separated them from the other nations, for God, by curing the disease, showed plainly as by an arm stretched out from heaven, that he approved of this kind of worship which they derived from the injunction of the law.[25]

So it is important that God be present in the Temple even in the time of Jesus, which is why Jesus himself performs a miracle of healing outside the Temple, for "it was no small ornament and glory of the temple, when God, by stretching out his hand, clearly showed that He was present."[26] Calvin also claims that Jesus teaches in the Temple to vivify the symbols of God's presence with the preaching of the Word, which is the soul of such symbols according to Calvin.[27] Jesus reassures the Jews of his day of the presence of God in the Temple by healing outside of the Temple itself, and endorses the legitimacy of worship in the Temple itself by teaching within it. Interestingly, these insights come from Calvin's commentary on the Gospel of John, which is often regarded as being more anti-Jewish than the Synoptic Gospels. The more toxic claims that Calvin makes about the Jews, cited in the previous chapter, come from Calvin's comments on the Synoptic Gospels. Whereas Calvin speaks in his John commentary of the presence of God in the Temple right at the time of Jesus, which is vivified by the actions of Jesus himself, he says in the harmony of the Gospels that God had already departed from the Temple owing to the sins of the people before Jesus ever arrived. These comments come two years after those on John. I have absolutely no idea what happened in his mind to harden his position so, but it really is quite a remarkable change in the way Calvin views the

---

[25] Comm. John 5:3, OE 11/1.152–53; CNTC 4:117.
[26] Ibid.
[27] Comm. John 7:14, OE XI/1, 234–35; CNTC 4:184–85.

Temple. But even though I am borrowing the evidence I want from John, I think there is a trajectory here that has a great deal of promise in giving us a more positive understanding of the presence of God in the Jewish community even after the death of Jesus.

Calvin clearly sees the importance of the presence of God among the Jews during and after the Babylonian exile in a way unlike any other theologian. He sees this as the decisive issue. Is God present among us or not? And even when in Babylon it looks like the answer is no, Calvin says Yes: the Temple still stands on the promise even though it is not visibly there, and God is with the people even in exile. Moreover, God restores the Temple in order to restore the people by dwelling in their midst, and continues to give signs of God's presence right up until the death of Jesus. Calvin even says that there was no need for the Temple to be destroyed after the coming of Christ, even though it would no longer have been the symbol of God's presence. "The Temple had indeed been built on the condition that at the coming of Christ, it would cease to be the abode and residence of deity, but it would have remained as a remarkable demonstration of the continued grace of God."[28] Calvin is pointing to a meaning of the symbols of God's presence that is not exhausted by the coming of Jesus Christ. Indeed, given the dynamic he creates from the Exodus through the restoration, it is very hard to see how there could be an end to the truthfulness of the symbols of God's presence in the Law, even after the coming of Christ. Why would there be? They are symbols of God's presence, and God has not gone anywhere. God pledges God's presence in the symbol, and God demonstrates God's presence by acting in concert with the symbol. Since God always remains like God, God is faithful to the promise to be present to the children of Abraham even when the symbols of God's presence are destroyed. Why would God act any differently in the future?

Now as we know, Calvin is convinced that the presence of God that was symbolized in all these ways, and that was truly present in

---

[28] Comm. Matthew 23:38, CO 45:644; CNTC 3:70.

all these ways in Israel's life, became fully manifested to us in Christ. So the God who is present in the Temple is now present to us in the One whom he calls "God manifested in the flesh" (1 Tim. 3:16). This is significantly a theo-centric definition of who Christ is. The same God is manifested in the flesh of Christ as had been manifested in the Temple. And the God who is manifested in the flesh of Christ is present to us now by the Holy Spirit, given with the symbols of Christ's presence in the Gospel, baptism, and the Holy Supper. So for Calvin, the God who was present to the Jews in the Temple is now present with Jews and Gentiles in Christ through the Holy Spirit, in a way that has freed us from the presence of God through the ceremonies of the law. All of this is of course a given for Calvin, and this is in fact Christianity. Paul tells us that if we want to reintroduce the ceremonies of the law, even circumcision, then we will lose the presence of God in Christ (Galatians 5:2). But the question with which Calvin leaves us is this: Does this mean that God cannot be present with the Jews anymore? Does the coming of Christ and the Christian belief that God is manifested in the flesh of Christ mean that God has decisively departed from the Jews? Is the presence of God a zero-sum game? Do the Jews have to lose God's presence in order for us to gain it in Christ? Calvin's assumption is, absolutely, the coming of God in Christ necessitates the departure of God from the symbols of the Law, so that God would no longer be present in the Temple even had it been allowed to remain standing. But is this accurate? Does this do justice to the biblical narrative Calvin is inviting us to read so carefully? Does this make any sense? Calvin would say, absolutely, because Titus came in and destroyed the Temple and destroyed Jerusalem and exiled the people and they have not been back. Moreover, this fulfills the divine decree revealed in Daniel, that there would be a second defilement of the Temple after that of Antiochus IV Epiphanes, and that would bring the final destruction of the people, as we saw in the previous chapter. So in his mind the answer is final: this is not Babylon again, this is the end. The Jews reject Christ because they cling to the Law of Moses, and so God rejects them in turn.

But is that, in fact, the case? What about the presence of God among the people in Babylon, even after the Temple had been destroyed? More importantly, what about Ezra? In order to answer this question in a more illuminating way, that can get us to see a trajectory coming out of the Bible which would explain why the Jews would essentially link the presence of God with the Law of Moses, we need to go back to the restoration of the Jewish people after Babylon and pay attention to an office that was created during the exile that did not exist before, that of the scribe. This office is absolutely pivotal for the life of the community after Babylon even unto today. Whatever the discontinuities may be between Ezra and Rabbinic Judaism, there is far more continuity than discontinuity between them so far as I can tell, which is why the Rabbis draw a line back from their own Sages to Ezra. In order to see the significance of Ezra, we need to consider the following question: When the Jews are taken into captivity, what is the lesson that God wants them to learn with regard to the presence of God in their midst? What was the point of destroying all the symbols of God's presence and taking the people away from the land, which was itself a symbol of God's presence? What were they supposed to learn from this experience? Calvin would say they tried to confine God to the symbols of God's presence, so God destroyed these symbols to show that God is free of them. God cannot be contained in the symbols of God's presence. However, I believe that Calvin is mistaken, perhaps because of his focus on the controversy with the Roman Church over the sacraments. The lesson Babylon was clearly meant to teach was that no matter how many promises God makes to you to be present to you, and no matter how unconditional those promises appear to be, you can never cling to those promises and neglect obedience to the Law of Moses. This is clearly the message delivered by the prophet Micah.

Hear this, you rulers of the house of Jacob and chiefs of the house of Israel, who abhor justice and pervert all equity, who build Zion with blood and Jerusalem with wrong! Its rulers give judgment for a bribe, its priests teach for a price, its prophets give oracles for money; yet they lean upon the Lord and say, "Surely the Lord is with us! No harm shall come upon us." Therefore because of you Zion shall be plowed as a field; Jerusalem shall become a heap of ruins, and the mountain of the house a wooded height. (Micah 3:9–12)

This is also the message delivered by the prophet Jeremiah many years later in the Temple in Jerusalem, when the Babylonians were already on the horizon.

Here you are, trusting in deceptive words to no avail. Will you steal, murder, commit adultery, swear falsely, make offerings to Baal, and go after other gods you have not known, and then come stand before me in this house, which is called by my name, and say, "We are safe!" – only to go on doing these abominations? (Jer. 7:8–10)

You cannot presume upon the promise that God will dwell in the Temple in order to oppress the poor and afflict the widow and grind the needy in the ground and think you are safe. You cannot commit murder and adultery and blasphemy and idolatry and violate the Law of Moses and then come into the Temple in which God's name dwells and think you will be saved. To teach you this, God will destroy the Temple as God destroyed Shiloh, and will cast you into Babylon. You cannot presume on God's presence. You must cling to God's law and obey it from your heart and teach it and observe it. And once Jerusalem is taken into captivity in Babylon, and the Temple is destroyed, the Jews knew beyond a shadow of a doubt that Micah and Jeremiah were right, that they had spoken the true message of God.

So it seems to me that if I were a Jew in Babylon, I would be seeking above all else to study the Law of Moses, and to teach this Law to all my people, so that every man, woman and child would study this law and apply this law to their life. Not to make God present, not to get God to forgive us, not to try to make ourselves worthy of being the people of God, but precisely because God is even now so graciously present, even as God had so graciously promised to be with us. Were God to graciously deliver us from Babylon and restore us miraculously to the land, how would we ever presume again to do any differently? So it is hardly a surprise that once the Temple is rebuilt, Ezra the Scribe of the Law appears. The Rabbis say that he waited to return to Jerusalem to demonstrate that obedience to the law and studying the law is more important than Temple sacrifice. Given the statements of Amos and Isaiah that God hates our feasts and despises our sacrifices, they clearly have a point. The law is the key. The promise of God to be present in our midst is true, the promise of God to be present in the Temple is true, and God has graciously acted to restore us to the land in spite of what our sins have deserved. But we must obey the Law of Moses to live in the presence of God. So Ezra comes back to Jerusalem with the law that he has studied and he teaches it. "This Ezra went up from Babylonia. He was a scribe skilled in the Law of Moses that the Lord the God of Israel had given" (Ezra 7:6). Calvin sees the importance of the rebuilding of the Temple at this time, but he misses the crucial role played by Ezra and the new office of the scribes, who attempt to address the essential relationship between the presence of God and the teaching of the law.

I am actually quite surprised that Calvin neglects Ezra, because Ezra sounds a lot like Calvin. The kind of office that Ezra creates, teaching the law and explaining it to the people so that they would apply it to their lives, looks a lot like the way Calvin and the other pastors of Geneva teach Scripture to all members of the congregation so that they might apply it to their lives. So I am surprised that Calvin did not take more interest in Ezra and his fellow scribes. Not that Ezra and Calvin teach the same thing – my whole point is that they do not – but rather the role they see for teachers in their respective communities is quite similar. In any case, the moment in this history that I find to be especially noteworthy comes after the Temple has been restored and the Levites have returned, so that the worship of the Temple might be restored. All of the people gathered as one person into the square before the Water Gate, and they told Ezra the Scribe to bring the book of the Law of Moses that the Lord had given to Israel.

> Accordingly, the priest Ezra brought the law before the assembly, both men and women and all who could hear with understanding. This was on the first day of the seventh month. He read from it facing the square before the Water Gate from early morning until midday, in the presence of the men and the women and those who could understand; and the ears of all the people were attentive to the book of the law. (Nehemiah 8:2–3)

Moreover, Ezra and his assistants not only read the law to the people but they also interpret the law for them, so that they understand what they are hearing. "So they read from the book, from the law of God, with interpretation. They gave the sense, so that the people understood the reading" (Nehemiah 8:8). This is remarkable. They read the book of the law for half a day, and then they interpret it, so that the people are not only attentive to the reading of the law, but are able to understand what they are hearing.

In response to the reading and interpretation of the law, the people gather in sackcloth to confess their sins and the sins of their ancestors, in one of the most remarkable prayers of confession in Scripture. They rehearse all of the gracious things that God had done on behalf of Israel, followed by an honest admission of the sinful and ungrateful response of the people, and the astonishing way God continued to forgive them and be present among them, right up to the captivity in Babylon. And they acknowledge that in spite of the gracious and forgiving ways of God, the fundamental problem was their failure to obey the Law of Moses. "You have been just in all that has come upon us, for you have dealt faithfully and we have acted wickedly; our kings, our officials, our priests, and our ancestors have not kept your law or heeded the commandments and the warnings which you gave them" (Nehemiah 9:33–34). In order to break this destructive cycle once and for all, the people as a whole make a covenant to obey the Law of Moses. "Because of all this, we make a firm agreement in writing, and on that sealed document are inscribed the names of our officials, our Levites, and our priests" (Nehemiah 9:38). They sign a covenant to observe and do all the commandments of the law given by Moses the servant of God, and enter into a curse lest they should disobey the law (Nehemiah 10:28–29). This moment is at least as important as the rebuilding of the Temple that Calvin highlights, and in many ways it is far more important, for Babylon reveals that the presence of God, though graciously promised, is inextricably linked to following the Law of Moses. In fact, I see this as the decisive moment in the history of the Jewish people after their return from Babylon, for it marks their explicit acknowledgement that the presence of God is intimately connected with the study and the observance of the Torah. It is to Calvin's credit that he gets us to read the Bible in this way. By raising up the restoration of the Jews in the presence of God in Jerusalem, he allows us to see what Christians almost never see, and what he himself appears not to see, namely, that the teaching of the Law of Moses is essential to the restoration of the Jews and to God's continued presence among them.

The permanent significance of this transition is accentuated by the crisis brought about by Antiochus IV Epiphanes. Calvin is well aware of this crisis, but understands it entirely in light of the defilement of the Temple, and not in terms of the Law. Antiochus persecutes the Jews who follow the law of Moses in an attempt to get them to accommodate themselves to the Greek way of life, thereby marking the first time in recorded history that people are tortured and executed solely for their religious beliefs and practices. Even though many Jews conform to Greek ways of life, there are many men, women, and children who are willing to be killed for the sake of the Law of Moses. Mothers have their sons circumcised knowing that they will be killed for doing so, and their sons killed too (2 Maccabees 6:10). Can you imagine circumcising your child knowing that it would bring the death of your child and your own death? They did so because they were convinced that God's presence was tied to their obedience to God's commandments. One mother watches as all seven of her sons are roasted alive before she herself is killed, all for refusing to disobey the Law of Moses. There were Jews hiding in the wilderness and the Seleucids pursued them, knowing that if they attacked them on the Sabbath, they would not fight back because they faithfully observed the Sabbath, and that is just what happened. They died to honor the Sabbath in which God is present (2 Maccabees 6:11). Most significantly for our purposes, one of the heirs of Ezra, the scribe Eleazar, is threatened with death if he does not eat pork. Some of the soldiers know him and offer to let him eat approved meat instead of pork, to spare his life. However, Eleazar categorically refuses, as he might lead astray the younger ones whom he taught for so many decades. "Therefore, by bravely giving up my life now, I will show myself worthy of my old age and will leave to the young a noble example of how to die a good death willingly and nobly for the revered and holy laws" (2 Maccabees 6:27–28). This story is retold in 3 and 4 Maccabees, right up to the time of Jesus, showing its significance during this period. This is astonishing to me, for it shows the depth of commitment to this new understanding of how the people would live in the presence of God, by being willing to die for the sake of the Law.

So the commitment to Ezra, and to what Ezra represents, is deep. People are willing to die for it. Yet such deep commitment to the Law of Moses is precisely what one would expect as being essential to the restoration of the Jews after Babylon. God remained faithful to the children of Abraham even when they disobeyed the Law of Moses. The Jews saw that they could only honor God's faithfulness by seeking faithfully to obey the Law in all things, so that they might continue to dwell in the presence of God. And this, in fact, is still the case. The presence of God is seen in Rabbinic thought to be directly tied to the study of the Torah. God is present whenever two gather to study the Torah; God is present whenever people observe the Torah; God is present in the observances of the feasts and the festivals as prescribed in Torah, and so on. This would be the expectation one would have coming out of this narrative if one were taught to read this narrative by none other than John Calvin, except that he forgot Ezra, or at most links Ezra to the restoration of the Temple.[29]

This leaves us, then, with a very perplexing situation, not perplexing to the Jews, mind you, but to the Christians. You have a situation in which, as Barth says, the Christian community owes the Jewish community everything. And you have a Jewish community which has enjoyed the presence of God from the dawn of its memory to now, in spite of incredible hardship, much of it caused by Christians – something that Barth and Calvin forget to mention, but that we need to remember. God is present among the Jews in an abiding and irrevocable way, and Christians simply need to get over it. It does not threaten Christian faith that this is true. I am not expecting a Jewish acknowledgement that God dwells among Christians, not only because we do not observe Torah, but especially given our treatment of the Jews for the past two thousand years. But a Christian acknowledgement that God has always dwelt with the Jews and dwells with the Jews now is long overdue, and can actually be quite a magnificent and liberating thing, for our very Scriptures lead us to make this acknowledgement. Indeed, Calvin himself makes this acknowledgement: "we consider that, for the sake of the promise, God's blessing still rests with them. For the apostle indeed testifies that it will never be completely taken away: 'For the gifts and the calling of God are without repentance' [Rom. 11:29, Vg.]."[30]

I want to conclude with an image of what this acknowledgment might look like in real life. My wife and I were blessed with the opportunity to visit the Gemarker Reformed Church of Wuppertal-Barmen in Germany this past spring. As you know, the church of Barmen was where the Barmen Declaration was signed, and it has six articles, none of which mention the Jews. Both Dietrich

---

[29] Comm. Isaiah 52:8, CO 37:248; CTS 16:101.
[30] Inst. IV.xvi.14, OS V.317–18; LCC 1337.

Bonhoeffer and Karl Barth were deeply disturbed by the fact that there was no seventh article of the Barmen Declaration denouncing Christian anti-Judaism and anti-Semitism once and for all. This omission also bothered the pastor of the church of Barmen, Karl Immer, who was himself a remarkable man. On the Sunday after Kristallnacht, during which the synagogue in Barmen was burned to the ground, Pastor Immer said that he would not preach, for a few hundred meters away the Word of God had been burned. So his passion for this question was much stronger, I think, than many of the theologians who were involved in the Barmen Declaration, and so the Barmen congregation felt this silence about the Jews quite profoundly, and wanted to address it.

Their chance came late in the twentieth century when several thousand Jews emigrated from Russia to the territory surrounding Barmen-Wuppertal in Westphalia. These Jews had no synagogue, and they put out a request to the city of Wuppertal-Barmen to help them acquire the land on which to build a synagogue. And so in the year 1997, the Gemarker Church at Barmen "wrote" what they consider to be Article VII of the Barmen Declaration. They tore down the rectory on their property and built a synagogue where it had stood, so that the synagogue is on the property of the church. The synagogue itself was dedicated in 2002. And so you have this astonishing reality, unique in the world, in which the Gemarker Church and the Barmen synagogue are on the same property in the center of the city. More remarkably – and this tells you where we are in this world today – they learned to their surprise that every single synagogue in Germany must be protected 24 hours a day, 365 days a year, by the police. A patrol must go around it once every two hours. Security cameras must be placed around it. It must be fenced. And so the church said, "If you must fence in the synagogue, then you must also place the church within the very same fence." So today one security fence goes around both the synagogue and the church.

However, more remarkably than that concrete act of solidarity, the church sees itself very clearly as honoring the presence of God in the synagogue, but they expect nothing in response. They can worship in the synagogue when invited, as is Jewish practice, but the Jews will not worship in the church, and the Christians neither want nor expect them to do so. The Gemarker Church acknowledges in this very concrete and visible way that the presence of God in the synagogue is unique, and they do not expect the synagogue to acknowledge the presence of God in the church. The wisdom of this church is astonishing, and the work they have done gives concrete form to the vision of the Jewish community I am trying to draw out of Calvin and Ezra. They see this. They acknowledge the uniqueness of the divine presence in the synagogue without asking for a reciprocal acknowledgement in return. So I will end this chapter with the image of this church and this synagogue side by side, protected by the same fence, but with a very clear distinction between them, in terms of how they understand each other.[31]

---

[31] For a full narration of this history, see Walter Lang, "The importance of the Barmen Declaration for the congregation in Wuppertal-Barmen today," *Ecumenical Review*, July 2009.

5 | The comfort and the challenge of love: John Calvin and Søren Kierkegaard

I would now like to consider how it is we come to know ourselves, and I will be bringing Søren Kierkegaard into conversation with John Calvin. I personally think that this is the most important element of the Christian life, and I love Calvin because he makes this theme an essential aspect of every theological topic. His basic conviction is that if you think you know God, but you do not come to know something about yourself thereby, you do not really know God. And if you think you know yourself, and you do not come to know something about God thereby, you do not really know yourself. Calvin is one of the rare figures I can think of in the Christian tradition that joins these two forms of knowledge together in a consistent way. And I am joining him, not surprisingly, with Søren Kierkegaard, who also viewed faith as a kind of transparency that rests in the power that established it, which is God. So both of them are very concerned to establish a kind of transparency of ourselves to ourselves before God. Rather alarmingly for both of them, we are already completely transparent to God. So human beings are already completely exposed to God, right down to our deepest secrets. The problem is that we are completely concealed from ourselves. So how do we go about becoming more and more transparent to ourselves? That is going to be the task for this chapter. I will start with Calvin's discussion of this, culminating in his description of the human being alone in conscience before the judgment seat of God. And the question I will ask, then, is: Can we really know ourselves before God's judgment? Will standing before the judgment seat of God, the tribunal of God, really allow us to become transparent to ourselves

before God? The segue to Kierkegaard will be Kierkegaard's asser-
tion that it is not God's judgment that allows us to become transparent to ourselves, because this transparency must be voluntary for
both theologians, but rather it is love. This means that the love of
God is simultaneously deeply terrifying and deeply consoling.

We will start with the many approaches Calvin takes to the knowledge of ourselves, for he is aware of the difficulty of this issue for
us, given that we are all too willing to deceive ourselves about ourselves. Calvin begins the *Institutes* with a description of wisdom.
He initially speaks in 1536 of true doctrine, but in later editions he
speaks of true wisdom, which I think is quite significant. He does
not say, "All our doctrine," but "All of our wisdom." My colleague
John Cavadini thinks a great deal about this. If you think about
theology as wisdom, it is a very different matter than approaching
theology as teaching or doctrine. John thinks that the early Church
teachers approached theology in this way, with Origen being one
of his favorites. I think that Calvin is following the early Church
teachers when he speaks about, "All of our wisdom." You often meet
people who are knowledgeable, but then you meet people who are
wise. The difference is that wisdom is knowledge that has tapped
into the depth of the life of the person. I think this is what Calvin is
trying to get us to see.

Moreover, all of our wisdom consists of two parts: knowledge of
God and knowledge of ourselves. We will be focusing on the knowledge of ourselves, but we will see that it is inextricably related to the
knowledge of God. Indeed, Calvin begins by saying that we cannot
know ourselves without simultaneously coming to know God. We
cannot descend into ourselves and see the benefits and the goodness
and the life and the powers of God about which we spoke in the
first chapter, and not immediately raise our thoughts to God – or at
least, we should not be able to do this – from whom all of these good
things flow. This is true even in the state of fallen humanity, for as
we have seen, the image of God remains within every person. There
is an abundance of goodness remaining in human beings vis-à-vis

this life. There may be no goodness remaining vis-à-vis eternal life, apart from faith in Christ, but we still need to be grateful for the benefits of this life, for our very life, he says, is nothing but a subsistence in the life of God. The very life we enjoy right now comes from our participation in the life of God. So one of the essential fruits of the knowledge of ourselves is gratitude. I think it is quite significant that Calvin does not get two sentences into the final edition of the *Institutes* before he starts describing the ascension of our heart from benefits we enjoy to the fountain of these benefits in God, which is the dynamic of gratitude.[1] So we truly know ourselves when we are grateful, even if this gratitude is confined to things that end in death. And these gifts are, for him, bounded by death.

There is another form of knowledge of ourselves which comes from our awareness of the "miserable ruin into which the revolt of the first person has plunged us."[2] So along with gratitude for what we enjoy now, there is a knowledge of ourselves that comes from knowing that humanity is no longer the way it was originally created to be. To know yourself in this way, you have to know something about what happened in Adam, which we will examine more fully below. But Calvin does not confine himself to Adam: he exhorts us to descend into ourselves, in order that we might feel the poverty and the evil things within ourselves. That is a very different thing than trying to see what happened to us in Adam, as we shall also see more fully below, for this is the self-knowledge everyone can come to themselves, even if they have never heard of Adam. You do not have to be told about Adam, or believe a particular doctrine of original sin; you only have to descend within yourself, and when you do so, you will be led to seek in God all of the good things of which you know yourself to be destitute. "To this extent we are prompted by our own ills to contemplate the good things of God; and we cannot aspire to him before we begin to become displeased with ourselves."[3] So there

---

[1] Inst. i.i.1, OS III.31–32; LCC 35–36.   [2] Inst. i.i.1, OS III.31.18–19; LCC 36.
[3] Inst. i.i.1, OS III.32.2–4; LCC 37.

are two forms of self-knowledge that lead to the knowledge of God: gratitude, which acknowledges God to be the source of the benefits we currently enjoy; and humility, which comes from the sense of our own poverty, and leads us to the acknowledgment that the good things of which we are destitute are to be sought only in God.

But Calvin knows how difficult it is for us truly to know ourselves, for we constantly deceive ourselves. Hence, "it is certain that man never achieves a clear knowledge of himself unless he has first looked upon God's face, and then descends from contemplating him to scrutinize himself."[4] Truly to know yourself, you must first contemplate the face of God and then descend into yourself, in order to consider yourself in relationship to God. As we saw in the second chapter, Calvin believes that we are created to be like God. We are created in the image of God to become more and more like God, so that we might be united to God. So when we contemplate the face of God, we must then immediately descend into ourselves and ask ourselves, how like God we are. And that, of course, is something only each one of us can answer. I like this element of Calvin, for he takes me away from considering other people in relationship to God – my spouse, my neighbor, my enemy – and brings me alone before the face of God, to descend into myself alone and compare myself to God. This contemplation will create an alarming situation in which we see more and more of the contradiction between the deeper part of our lives and the nature of God, but for Calvin, that is really the only way we can come to know ourselves. "Hence that dread and wonder with which Scripture commonly represents the saints as stricken and overcome whenever they felt the presence of God."[5]

However, later in the *Institutes*, at the beginning of his discussion of the knowledge of God the Redeemer, Calvin adds another form of contemplation by which we come to know ourselves. He claims that we come to know ourselves as we are now by comparing

[4] Inst. I.i.2, OS III.32.10–12; LCC 37.
[5] Inst. I.i.3, OS III.33.13–15; LCC 38–39.

ourselves to our originally created nature. In order to follow this form of contemplation, we first have to know how we were originally created to be in Adam, and then compare ourselves to our state in the present. In other words, one form of the knowledge of ourselves leads to another form of the knowledge of ourselves, which is something for which he does not account at the beginning of the *Institutes*, for there he speaks of how we come to the knowledge of God from the knowledge of ourselves, or the knowledge of ourselves from the knowledge of God. But here we move from a knowledge of ourselves as originally created, to a knowledge of ourselves as fallen. "But that primal worthiness cannot come to mind without the sorry spectacle of our foulness and dishonor presenting itself by way of contrast, since in the person of the first man we have fallen from our original condition."[6]

Calvin claims that when we compare ourselves as fallen with ourselves as created, we will discover that we were created with an immortal essence, which is our soul. "In the beginning God fashioned us after his image [Gen. 1:27] that he might arouse our minds both to zeal for virtue and to meditation on eternal life."[7] This is where Calvin is vastly different from virtually all of us these days. Calvin was convinced that the meaning of human life is to be found only in eternity. The meaning of human life is eternity. We were created for eternity, and the immortal soul reveals this destiny to us. Our soul has this immortality only by participation in God, but our soul reveals to us that our destiny is union with God. Our goal is not to be found in this world, but only in God. And so Calvin would be very upset with us, for we rarely talk about this anymore, and may not even believe that the destiny and goal of humanity is eternity, is union with God. We are very focused, for understandable reasons, on the ills of this life or the good things of this life, but Calvin would want us to focus primarily on God, for our creation in the image of

---

[6] Inst. ii.i.1, OS iii.229.1–5; LCC 242.
[7] Inst. ii.i.1, OS iii.228.29–31; LCC 242.

God was to orient us entirely in that direction. So the comparison of our current nature with our nature as originally created will reveal to us the misery of our current state, for we now find ourselves bounded by corruption, suffering, and death. Death in particular reveals to Calvin the loss of our original life, which was to end in eternity. So one thing we should feel profoundly is that we were created for immortality, and yet, through sin, death has entered the world, so we are now subject to death. We will also come to know that we are powerless to overcome the power of death and corruption. So we become aware of the calamity into which we have fallen in Adam, and of our utter impotence to do anything about it. This is the goal of comparing ourselves as created to ourselves as fallen.

> First, he should consider for what purpose he was created and endowed with no mean gifts. By this knowledge he should arouse himself to meditation on divine worship and the future life. Secondly, he should weigh his own abilities – or rather, lack of abilities. When he perceives this lack, he should lie prostrate in extreme confusion, so to speak, reduced to naught.[8]

True knowledge of ourselves gives rise to humility, which is rooted in the sense of our own nothingness. However, Calvin does not want us to be crushed by this humility, but rather to be led by it to seek God yet again from the depth of our heart. "From this source arise abhorrence and displeasure with ourselves, as well as true humility; and thence is kindled a new zeal to seek God, in whom each of us may recover those good things which we have utterly and completely lost."[9] Calvin wants us in humility to flee to God as the source of the goodness we now lack. So genuine humility always refers us to God. I think this is extremely important, not only for Calvin, but also for Kierkegaard. There are destructive ways of talking about humility. There are ways of speaking about our virtual nothingness

---

[8] Inst. II.i.3, OS III.231.5–11; LCC 244.

[9] Inst. II.i.1, OS III.229.5–8; LCC 242.

before God that do not, in fact, lead us to seek God. They just make us feel utterly destitute of all hope. That is never Calvin's intent, and that is certainly never Kierkegaard's intent. The sense of humility and the sense of poverty and the sense of our sin and our death are meant to lead us to seek from the depth of our heart the goodness that is found only in God. That is always the goal for Calvin, the relationship to God.

However, Calvin is aware that we human beings are constantly misjudging ourselves by comparing ourselves to each other. We take the standard of our knowledge of ourselves not from the face of God that we contemplate, or humanity as originally created, but rather how we look compared to others. Our knowledge of ourselves based on such comparison leads us to seek status in comparison to others. We are constantly seeking enhanced status in the human community, and we are desperate when such status is not given, or when it is given to someone to whom we feel superior, as when an honor goes to a colleague when you really think it should have gone to you – it is devastating. And when an honor comes to you that you really think should have come to you, it is exalting, it is wonderful, it is inflating. So we are constantly diverting ourselves from descending into ourselves by consoling ourselves that we really are not all that bad compared to others. The minute we start to sense that something is really amiss with ourselves, Calvin thinks that we start looking around and comparing ourselves to others. And we comfort ourselves by saying, Well, I might be bad, but she is a lot worse! We see this especially in relation to our bodies and our physical appearance. We may be concerned that we have gained too much weight, but we console ourselves by thinking, Well, I might be heavy, but look at that person! He is really heavy! And of course that person is also looking around trying to find somebody even heavier than he is, and if you wind up being the heaviest person in the room, God help you.

Calvin claims that this tendency to come to know ourselves in comparison to others reveals the frightening extent of our hypocrisy and self-love. "For, such is the blindness with which we all rush into self-love that each one of us seems to himself to have just cause to be proud of himself and to despise all others by comparison."[10] If we become aware of our faults, we hide them from others and exaggerate their faults. If we are aware of the superior gifts of others, we belittle them in order to feel better about ourselves. Calvin is convinced that the only way to overcome such refusal to descend into ourselves is to awaken our conscience, for it is only the conscience that can illuminate the deepest recesses of our hearts, of our souls, of our minds. The awakened conscience will finally succeed in overcoming your tendency to compare yourself to others by focusing your attention entirely on yourself. Calvin has a very precise definition of conscience that he gives in the *Institutes*: he calls it "a sense of divine judgment."[11] He gets this definition from the meaning of the word itself in Latin: for conscience means "to know with." And his question is, with whom does the conscience know? And the answer is, God. Conscience is your knowledge of God's judgment of you. So if you rightly tap into the conscience, which everyone has and so everyone can do, you can become aware right now of God's judgment of you, including God's eschatological judgment of you. God is already judging each one of us, and the conscience is God's way of sharing that knowledge with us. Conscience is the way God already sees us, and if we awaken our conscience and learn to see ourselves through our conscience, we can come to see ourselves the way God already sees us, and we become revealed to ourselves.

Calvin is especially interested in how the conscience reveals the secret thoughts of the heart, following Paul's description in Romans 2:14–16. According to Calvin, only God can penetrate into the depths of our hearts, and so our participation in God's judgment can lead us into the deepest, darkest secret recesses of our heart. Calvin is vividly aware of the many ways we deceive ourselves, of the deep ways we lie to ourselves, of the ways we construct a persona that we

---

[10] Inst. III.vii.4, OS IV.154.12–15; LCC 693.

[11] Inst. III.xix.15, OS IV.295.12; LCC 848.

RECONSIDERING JOHN CALVIN

really want others to believe to hide from them who we really are. We may even come to believe that the persona is who we really are. And once we fool others, and even fool ourselves, we think that we can fool God, hiding from God behind the persona we have created. "And yet hypocrites would tread these twisting paths so as to seem to approach the God from whom they flee."[12] So we come to think that God will believe that the mask we have created is who we really are. We construct a pious persona of wonder and awe and love and gentleness, to hide the fact that inside we are filled with resentment and grudges and bitterness. We act as though we love others, including those closest to us, but inside we keep score every time our loved ones do not do the dishes when they should have, or they do not clean the bathroom, or when we think they have slighted us in the smallest way. They irritate the hell out of us, and we talk to ourselves about them all the time, even as we smile on the outside and say that everything is fine, that we truly love each other.

The most dangerous time for all of this is when we assemble to worship God, for Calvin is aware that in worship human beings become inveterate liars. It is the most dangerous moment in human life because we all become hypocrites, we all become what we think the Church wants us to be, what God wants us to be, what our neighbors want us to be. We are not ourselves. "Irreligious men, although they often resort to the sacred assemblies, frequent them merely as lurking places, where they may escape the eye of God."[13] It is astonishing to me that Calvin sees this so clearly, that church is the most perilous place in our lives, because when we get to church, the danger is that everyone may be acting. It is a theater, and we all know the role we are to play. "Good morning, pastor! Oh, have a nice day!" But inside we are already keeping tabs of all the things the pastor did wrong, of all the ways our fellow Christians are failing, of all the ways that our worship together drives us crazy, of how hard it is to

---

[12] Inst. I.iv.4, OS III.44.4–5; LCC 50–51.
[13] Comm, Psalm 26:8, CO 31:268B; CTS 8:382.

pray when surrounded by people whom we hate. To expose us as actors, Calvin always focuses his attention on the inmost thoughts of the heart, for he is aware of the conversations within conversations that we have. I have actually heard of a play in which the actors say on stage what their characters are really thinking – not what they are supposed to be thinking, but what they really think about other people, and it is, as you can imagine, excruciating to watch. There was an episode on the TV show *House* with a similar theme. A man who appeared to be a happy husband and father acquired a disease in which he could not keep himself from saying what he really thought about those whom he loved., and of course it ruined every relationship in which he was involved. When he said what he really thought, his wife hated him, his daughter hated him, even House, who is a very difficult person himself, hated him. They desperately wanted him to go back to the way he was, when he did not say what he thought, but when he said what he knew they wanted to hear. If he went back to being an actor, to being a liar, they could love him again, but not when he spoke the truth.

We all do this, we all have a conversation within ourselves that is deeply hidden from the world, and at the same time there is another conversation that we have externally that is completely unrelated to the internal conversation, and we can carry on these two conversations at exactly the same time. I have thought about doing a comic strip in which to show this phenomenon visually. One professor would be saying to his colleague, "Oh, hi Randall, how is your work going?" while the interior bubble would show him saying, "Are you writing another lightweight book? Or are you too busy watching *House*?" And then I would reply, "Oh Tom, I'm doing great!" while inside I am saying, "Still writing your students' papers for them so they all get As?" And then he would say, "By the way, congratulations on winning that endowed Chair," while inside he is saying, "Even though you have done nothing to deserve it, and everyone knows it should have been given to me!" And so it goes on and on. Calvin is vividly aware of the things we do to fool each other, and we do fool each other. We can even deceive a whole community, in fact we do this all the time. That is why serial killers and spouse abusers often hide in plain sight by enthusiastically attending church, and by being prominent and well-respected members of their churches. And people will say, "Well, he could not be the BK Killer because he is an upstanding member of the Lutheran Church, and we know his family, and they are wonderful members, too." And all the while he is out there killing women every other week, while he hides in church. This would not surprise Calvin at all. He knows that church is a very dangerous place.

This is something I need to think about, that we all need to think about. Why are churches encouraging falsehood? Why are churches encouraging lies? Why are churches encouraging hypocrisy? We do this all the time. We have very clear expectations of the people with whom we worship. I am an Episcopalian, so I know how this works! And if you cannot conform to these expectations, then you might as well not bother coming back. You cannot appear in the wrong clothes, or fumble with your hymnal and prayer book and bulletin, or make a lot of noise – it is a matter of decorum! There is a story that I heard on NPR, of a Methodist minister who became an alcoholic, which is a besetting sin of clergy, Protestant and Roman Catholic, and he went into recovery after he almost died from alcohol. And after he recovered, he opened a recovery ministry in Minneapolis, Minnesota, which had as its ministerial focus people with drinking problems, which meant that it was not exactly in the nice part of town. And his church attracted many people who had never before darkened the door of a church, or if they had, they soon left, for they felt judged and excluded, as though they had to hide who they really were. When the reporter asked one member what was special about this church, he said that it was incredible, he never thought church could be like this. And she said, "Why?" And he replied, "I can come to church and be honest. I am a broken human being who drinks too much, and I cannot stop it. And when I come to this church, I can admit this to myself and everyone else." It is astonishing to me that this minister had the openness to do this, but he clearly knew that he himself was broken, and so he could actually have a congregation in which people were encouraged to openly acknowledge who they really were. The one place in the world they could go to be honest was that church. And both they and the reporter knew how rare this is, which is why they did the story about it on NPR. So we need to ask ourselves, why are our churches encouraging people to be actors, to be liars, to be dishonest with themselves and with others?

The other difficulty we have, of course, is that the secrets we conceal from others are sometimes hidden from ourselves. There are things we will not admit to other people, or most other people, then there are things we will admit to our closest friends, then there are things we might admit to a spouse, but then there are things we will not even admit to ourselves, for when we catch a glimpse of them, we run away, and cannot bear to look. But that is precisely where Calvin wants us to go. What is the secret part of your soul that you have locked up and guarded so carefully and camouflaged as something else; that you will not even open in private because it is so toxic? What is that secret, buried deep within you that you will not even talk about with yourself? You think it is safely hidden, but it affects your whole personality, and it is going to ruin everything. And Calvin knows that unless the conscience can shine its light in there, which it is trying to do, then we cannot come to know ourselves, whereas once we can admit that secret, then we really do know ourselves. Calvin knows how difficult it is to awaken the conscience to such a degree that it can get us to see these things, and that is really my question for this chapter. How is this actually possible? How is it possible to open up that part of ourselves and constantly to examine ourselves so that we are always seeking this kind of transparency?

Calvin has many suggestions as to how to do this, one of which is, as you know, the law of God, an idea which he clearly derives from Martin Luther. Calvin claims that the law of God is given to us first of all so that we might compare ourselves to the law in our conscience. For the law reveals to us what the image of God looks like. "For God has so depicted his character in the law that if any man carries out in deeds whatever is enjoined there, he will express the image of God, as it were, in his own life."[14] If your life expresses the law, then you truly image God. So the law is a divinely revealed portrait of what your life should look like. Moreover, it is both an image and a mirror. It is an image holding before you the character of God that your life is to resemble, and it is a mirror because you can see yourself reflected in it, so that you can compare yourself with the prototype that you see. So you are to look at the image in the mirror and then look at yourself and see yourself in comparison to it. "The law is like a mirror. In it we contemplate our weakness, then the iniquity arising from this, and finally the curse coming from both – just as a mirror shows us the spots on our face."[15] Calvin thinks that if you do this rightly, your conscience will accuse you, not only of being in total contradiction to that image, but also of being powerless to do anything about it. This in turn will humble you in the knowledge of your sin, and lead you to seek what you lack in God. "This means that, dismissing the stupid opinion of their own strength, they come to realize that they stand and are upheld by God's hand alone; that, naked and empty-handed, they flee to his mercy, repose entirely in it, hide deep within it, and seize upon it alone for righteousness and merit."[16] Without this prototype and mirror, our conscience is powerless to break through the layers of self-deception we have created for ourselves. "Besides this, he is so puffed up with haughtiness and ambition, and so blinded by self-love, that he is as yet unable to look upon himself and, as it were, to descend within himself, that he may humble himself and confess his own miserable condition."[17] So Calvin thinks that the law awakens the conscience, if you will, to do its job.

---

[14] Inst. II.viii.51, OS III.390.16–20; LCC 415.
[15] Inst. II.vii.7, OS III.332.33–36; LCC 355.
[16] Inst. II.vii.8, OS III.334.15–21; LCC 357.
[17] Inst. II.viii.1, OS III.344.20–23; LCC 368.

But there is still a problem with looking to the law to awaken the conscience, and living in Indiana, I know this first hand. The law, unfortunately, has now become a weapon to be used against others. In Indiana, there are many Christians who want to put the Ten Commandments everywhere because other people's lives are really screwed up, so if you just put the Ten Commandments out there then those people who are really messed up will get straightened out. The problems in our society are all caused by the fact that we do not have the law displayed prominently in front of our schools and courthouses. So we need to display the law so that other people can come to see what a horrible mess they have made out of their lives, and in doing so we feel so much better about ourselves by comparison. So the law can be a dangerous thing, for there is no guarantee that I will not make the law serve my attempt to know myself in comparison with others. I think Calvin underestimates how much this could happen, and this has become one of the besetting sins of American Protestantism. We have this magical idea that if you just put the Ten Commandments up in a courthouse or on a lawn or some other public place, everyone is going to go, "Oh wow! Really?! I did not know God disapproved of murder! If that is the case, I will definitely not kill any more. Sorry about that!" This approach is astonishing naive, but it is also outwardly directed, so that the law no longer awakens my conscience. We have learned how to use a mirror that was meant to lead us to descend into ourselves to see the deepest secrets we are concealing from ourselves and one another, so that it becomes a weapon we use against others, to tell other people to get their act in gear. So the law does not really work, for it does not keep us from comparing ourselves to others, and as long as we are allowed to make comparison with others, we are always going to be diverting ourselves from coming to know ourselves. We are never really going to descend within ourselves. We are always going to be looking at others and saying, "Yeah, well I might be a sinner, but at least I am not as bad as she is!"

Calvin thinks that the law will ultimately do its job, the knowledge of Adam will do its job, the conscience itself will do its job if it brings me alone before God, so that I see myself alone before God, as God really sees me. At its core the conscience always brings the person alone before God. So right now you are alone before God, and God already sees you right down to the hidden depths of your heart. According to Calvin, the way God sees us is exactly opposite to the way that we come to see others. We see from the outside, and we work our way gradually in, and sometimes we never have a clue of what truly lies hidden at the core. There are cultures that are very skilled at this kind of concealment. I learned this in Alaska from the Inuit, although others have learned this from other Native American cultures. The Eskimos know how to fool westerners by initiating them into a false intimacy. If you spend time with them and get to know them, you learn things that others from the lower forty-eight do not know, and so you think to yourself, "Wow, I am really getting to know the Eskimos." You know, for a liberal Protestant like me, it is a wonderful thing to feel that I am down with the Eskimos! But the whole time, I am so far above what is really going on that I would not even know I was missing anything unless they told me. I finally got to know them well enough that they told me that the heart of their culture was completely hidden from me, but they of course told me nothing about what it was that I still did not know about them. It made me sad to realize that we westerners have made this kind of concealment a necessary strategy of survival for native peoples. So there are cultures that can fool you into thinking you know them intimately, but you do not. But we do this with ourselves, too; we think we know ourselves and we do not. But God actually sees us in the opposite way. God sees us from the inside out. So God sees us from that deepest secret part of ourselves first, and then sees everything out from there. And if you can learn to see yourself that way, you can learn to see yourself the way God already sees you. You learn to see yourself from the inside out, from the bottom up, if you will, from the depth on out. You do not do an archaeological dig down from the persona to the secrets of the heart, but start from the secrets of the heart and work up from there.

Calvin thinks that the conscience is already there, in the deepest recess of your soul. It sees your secret thoughts already. And you know it does. You know it does because these thoughts that you have just bother you, and may wake you up in the middle of the night. You ask yourself, "Why do I keep thinking these incredibly awful things about people I love, and about God, and about others?" Therefore, if we really are to know ourselves, we must be hailed in conscience before the judgment seat of God. And when that happens, you are there all alone, in solitude before God. This, actually, is the Reformation, if you think about it. The Reformation was a cry for every person to realize that no one else can answer for you. When God calls you to account, you have to answer. Luther thought the moment at which this happens is the hour of your death, when you will most certainly be alone. And when God summons you before God's tribunal to give an account of your life, no one will be able to answer for you – the pastor cannot answer for you, the pope cannot answer for you, the community cannot answer for you, even Luther cannot answer for you. You have to stand alone before God and answer. And the question is, how will you answer? You must answer. She cannot answer for you, they cannot answer for you, you must answer. And God is not going to wait around until you form a committee and get back to God later. No, you must answer. So we need to train ourselves for this time, Calvin thinks, and realize that we always stand alone before the tribunal of God. We are always being asked how we will stand before this tribunal.

The process of descending into ourselves in conscience is learning that we are always alone before God, being asked to give an accounting of our lives. So we need to practice this in our daily lives, to descend from the contemplation of God's judgment seat into the secret recesses of our hearts, to reveal the wickedness which otherwise lies too deeply hidden. I think this is really the most promising avenue Calvin takes with regard to the knowledge of ourselves, when he reminds us that we are already alone before God in our conscience, so that we might come to see ourselves, or try to see ourselves, the way God sees us. Since God already sees us that way, it is possible for us to learn to see ourselves the way God sees us. But notice that when this happens, you are not seeing anyone else. God is not asking me about anyone else. God is asking me about myself, that is all. The minute you start thinking of someone else, you know you are on the wrong track. So this is the question Calvin would have us contemplate: "How shall we reply to the Heavenly Judge when he calls us to account?"[18] How will we answer? Without keeping this question in mind, we do not know what it means to descend into ourselves truly to know ourselves. "In short, this whole discussion will be foolish and weak unless every man admit his own guilt before the Heavenly Judge, and concerned about his own acquittal, willingly cast himself down and confess his nothingness."[19] The key here is that the confession of your nothingness before God is voluntary. You voluntarily humble yourself before God and confess your nothingness. It is also important to notice that you are doing this alone, and you are doing this before God. You are not making yourself nothing before other people. That is what we try to avoid at all cost, so that we can feel like we are something by comparison with other people. And being humbled and made to feel like nothing before others is not the kind of self-knowledge Calvin seeks, for this is likely as false as other forms of self-deception. No, you voluntarily confess your nothingness before God.

On the other hand, living with an awakened conscience before God may actually make you into something quite astonishing in relation to other people. A person with this kind of a conscience is the kind of person with whom you want to be, because they are always before God. Unlike other people, who avoid sinning because they might get caught, or because others might think badly of them,

---

[18] Inst. III.xii.1, OS IV.208.14–15; LCC 755.
[19] Inst. III.xii.1, OS IV.209.15–17; LCC 756.

the person of conscience will avoid sin because she would never seek to violate her relationship with God. Even if they were on a desert island, they would not sin, because God sees everything. And so a human being who sees herself the way God sees her is the most trustworthy, the most reliable, the most loving person you could know, for she will continue to love even when all others begin to hate. Calvin's hope is that if we learn how to do this, we would actually become what it means to be a human being, even if that leads us to humble ourselves and to confess our nothingness before God. This does not sound like good news, but actually it is tremendously liberating, because that secret down in there that we are hiding tells us that we are nothing, in spite of our best efforts to make ourselves something. And that is why we hide it, because we want to be something. So when we let that go, when we let it go and see it for what it is, it is actually liberating, even in the humility, and it is exalting, even in the nothingness.

But my question is, is this description of conscience really adequate? Can we really stand before the judgment seat of the Creator, the tribunal of God, and willingly confess our sin and our nothingness? Will not the sense of God's judgment cause us to seek to hide, so that we will not open ourselves fully before God? Calvin knows this, and actually explicitly acknowledges in some places, that unless you know already the love of God, you will never do this, you will run. The sense of judgment will still lead us to lie, or lead us to hide. After all, it was their alarmed consciences that made Adam and Eve run, their awakened consciences that made them hide. "Adam, where are you?" It may well be the alarmed conscience that makes us clothe ourselves in all these different ways. And so the question becomes whether there is a way of understanding this dynamic of coming to the knowledge of ourselves that avoids the possibility that it would not work, that you would be so afraid of the divine Judge that you would not voluntarily humble yourself and confess your nothingness. Can we really become transparent to ourselves before God's judgment?

I would like to explore another alternative to the knowledge of ourselves that actually begins where Calvin leaves off, namely, being alone before God in conscience. This brings us once again to Søren Kierkegaard. Søren Kierkegaard loved the idea of Confession. And he actually has a very traditional view of confession where you would go alone before God to a priest without a confessional; by the way, he knew the history of the practice of confession pretty well. He knew that in Luther's time you would go to a priest one on one in silence, all alone, and you would confess your sin to that person. Luther confessed by kneeling next to von Staupitz, his confessor, and confessed his sins face to face. It was very intimate; Staupitz was sitting right there. After the Reformation, rumors start to occur that women are going too frequently to confess, and the priest looks a lot happier afterwards, so they put the confessional out in the sanctuary. It used to be a very quiet, very secluded, very peaceful, very still place. Now they put it out in the hubbub of the sanctuary, and then you go there. And you are in a box and the priest is in a box, which already creates distance. You are already safer there than you were before, when confession took place face to face, for now a screen separates you. Then the Danish Lutheran Church thought that was too much – it was too much like the papacy, and so they created a service of confession in which you gather together with the pastor outside of the worship service and confess your sins in silence before God, and then the pastor says some words of comfort, and this allows you to go to Communion. And Kierkegaard thinks, well isn't this interesting? Confession becomes more and more impersonal, more and more public and corporate. "The abolition of Confession [is] the joint action of congregation and clergy. The congregation became afraid of going to confession; the confessional box brought matters too close to home. The clergy became afraid of hearing confession; things became much too earnest."[20]

[20] *Søren Kierkegaard's Journals and Papers*, vol. 1, A–E, ed. and trans. Howard V. Hong and Edna H. Hong (Bloomington and London: Indiana University Press, 1967), 242.

But what he likes about confession even in his own day is that you voluntarily withdraw yourself from the crowd in order to stand before God in silence. You are quiet, you are still. There is stillness in the moment of Confession, even with the pastor and other people around, for when you come before God to confess your sin, you are alone. You find yourself in solitude even when others are present, for you are opening yourself before God to come to know and confess your sin. This time is absolutely essential, he thinks, to knowing yourself. So the beginning of self-knowledge for Kierkegaard is stillness, and the alternative to that is busyness. And I think he is right. Kierkegaard senses in the nineteenth century that human status is achieved in many ways in our culture by how busy we are. When somebody asks us if they can meet us for lunch, there is nothing better than to say, "Oh, God, I am really busy. I am just so busy that I do not have time to talk to you right now, let alone have lunch with you. I just have so many things to do!" You see, that elevates us in the other's eyes. On the other hand, if I respond to such a request by saying, "Yes, I could talk to you right now, I could make a moment of utter stillness and solitude for us right here," you would say, "He does not do anything! This guy has nothing but time! I thought he was important." Our culture places a high value on being busy, on being productive, on rushing from one thing to the next, on never having time for anything.

Kierkegaard also knew that the nineteenth century was enamored of the crowd. It liked noise. It liked crowds. It judged the importance of an event by how many people were there. If only two people took to the street to protest, that was nothing; but if tens of thousands showed up, and made quite a bit of noise, why even the king would have to step down, as in fact happened in 1848. He would not be surprised by our own day, when we take polls to find out how people think, when we count votes, when we are impressed by large numbers of people or large percentages of voters. How many tens of thousands of people were there? How much noise did they make? I know all about this at Notre Dame, where we pack our stadium with 86,000 people and get them all to scream, "We are ND!" to intimidate our opponents with the size of our crowd and the volume of our noise. We love the crowd, we love the noise, and so we do not care all that much about solitude, about silence. In fact, we work very hard to avoid being silent or alone. If we must be alone, and cannot be busy, we will turn on the television, or put on an iPod, or play with our cell phone, or stare at the Internet. So stillness, silence, is something we do not value at all.

Kierkegaard knows that if we are to come to know ourselves, we must split ourselves off from the crowd, we must withdraw from the noise, and one place he thought we could do this is the moment of Confession. In that stillness, in that solitude, you can finally start to hear something you otherwise drown out with all the noise. You can start to hear the voice of conscience, which for him is the voice of eternity, the voice of God. So the first thing Kierkegaard asks us to do is to become completely still, so that we are no longer busy, no longer part of the crowd, for those are the ways we distract ourselves and delude ourselves, so that we never become transparent to ourselves. And in this stillness he thinks we can start to hear the voice of conscience. He asks, then, what is conscience? And he says in conscience, it is God who looks at a person, so that now in everything the person must look to God.[21] This is remarkably similar to Calvin. For both theologians, God is already looking at you in your conscience, and in the stillness you can start to look at God, which we rarely do. We are always looking at something else, but now we have to stop and look at God. And this conscience, which represents God looking at us, is our God-relation, as he calls it, "because to relate to God is precisely to have a conscience."[22] So when in stillness you discover your conscience, you discover that you are related to God, "because the relationship between the individual and God, the God-relationship, is the conscience."[23]

[21] Søren Kierkegaard, *Works of Love*, ed. and trans. Howard V. Hong and Edna H. Hong (Princeton University Press, 1995), 377.
[22] Ibid., 143.   [23] Ibid.

Once you discover the God-relation in conscience, you also discover that this relation, as Calvin also points out, is yours alone. No one else has this relationship to God; this is your relationship to God. No one else is responsible for this relationship to God; you alone are responsible before God for who you are, for what you are, for whether you know yourself. No one should or could step in at this point. "Each man himself, as an individual, should render his account to God. No third person dares venture to intrude upon this accounting between God and the individual."[24] I think Kierkegaard is right about this, and I think Calvin knows he is right, but one of the things that Calvin does, and his reputation precedes him in this, is that he intrudes on this relationship. He does not trust the individual to stand alone before God in conscience, for he does not think we will learn what we need to know. So he will teach you about your fallenness, and show that it started in Adam. He will present you with his theory of what happened to you in Adam, and he will teach you his doctrine of human corruption, to reveal to you what is wrong with you. And when he does this, I think that his readers rightly sense that something has gone wrong. We feel that he is prying, that he is too interested in my life, too concerned to show me that he is right about me.

But you see, Calvin is hardly alone. This is what we all do. We all get in the way of each person's relationship to God. We all know better than that person does what is really supposed to be going on in their relationship with God. And so rather than attend to my relationship to God in my conscience – which is highly problematic and highly challenging, utterly surprising and threatening at the same time – I start getting really interested in somebody else's relationship to God. And I want them to know just how sinful, or how good; how awful, or how wonderful they are in the eyes of God. But I have no business there. That is not my job. That is God's business, God's concern.

---

[24] Søren Kierkegaard, *Purity of Heart Is To Will One Thing*, trans. Douglas V. Steere (New York: Harper Torchbooks, 1956), 185.

"After all, what is eternity's accounting other than that the voice of conscience is forever installed with its eternal right to be the exclusive voice?"[25] By attending to our own relationship with God in our conscience, we can make other people aware that they are also responsible before God, but that is all we can do. All we can do is live this way. And I do think Calvin creates problems for himself, and diverts us from the task of becoming transparent before God in conscience, by creating general arguments about human sinfulness with which we can then argue. We can say, "That is not what happened in Adam!" But who really knows what happened in Adam? It is a really short story that does not have a lot of theology in it, you know? So you can argue until the cows come home about what happened in Adam, and never, ever, ever come to descend within yourself in conscience, never see yourself as accountable before God. You can just argue to death about original sin or original blessings and never see that you are already alone before God in your conscience, that God is already speaking with you in your conscience, to reveal you to yourself. "Eternity seizes each one by the strong arm of conscience, holding him as an individual. Eternity sets him apart with his conscience."[26]

Kierkegaard therefore has a profound suspicion of the people who want to get between you and God and tell you what is going on in your relationship to God. He thinks that all of us suspect that there is something wrong with this arrangement. To their credit, Barth and Bonhoeffer both seriously objected to the turn in modern Protestant theology which sought to tell people who thought they were happy that they were really filled with dread, with Angst. "You think you are happy, but you are really anxious." They thought that we should not meddle in that way, as our meddling corrodes the trust that others might have in us. We think we know better, and we think we have the right and the obligation to tell people what is wrong with them, and that is the problem. We need to be alone, since our conscience is talking to us about ourselves alone.

[25] Ibid., 186.   [26] Ibid., 192.

Moreover, like Calvin, Kierkegaard thinks that our conscience makes us completely transparent before God. God is already looking at us in our conscience, and God already sees right through us. "But before God [we] were and are continually single individuals; the person sitting in a showcase is not as embarrassed as every human being is in his transparency before God. This is the relationship of conscience."[27] So we are already transparent before God and our conscience is that relationship of transparency. The problem is that we are not transparent to ourselves. The true preacher of repentance, therefore, who reveals to me my own relationship to God, is my own conscience. "Deep within every person's heart, there dwells his preacher of repentance. If he speaks, he does not preach to others, he does not make you into a preacher of repentance – he preaches only to you."[28] Kierkegaard wants us to listen to this preacher of repentance, and ignore the preachers who preach repentance to us in stern and terrifying tones. "Therefore do not be afraid of the preacher of repentance who perhaps has terror in his countenance and wrath in his voice, who scolds and castigates and thunders. All that is just a game, and becomes merely a kind of shuddering entertainment."[29] This kind of preaching is just a theatrical performance. It may be highly effective, by the way, as we can see in the religiosity of the United States, which has been shaped by revivalism and its gripping preaching of repentance. Kierkegaard knew this himself through the Pietism in which his father raised him. But he thinks that it is just a game, even if it is one that makes us shudder. Do not pay any attention to them. You are assigned a preacher of repentance, and that preacher of repentance preaches only to you about your unique relationship with God. That is the voice to which you need to listen because it is a voice unique to every one of us, and it is going to say

---

[27] Søren Kierkegaard, *The Sickness unto Death*, ed. and trans. Howard V. Hong and Edna H. Hong (Princeton University Press, 1980), 124.

[28] Søren Kierkegaard, *Christian Discourses*, ed. and trans. Howard V. Hong and Edna H. Hong (Princeton University Press, 1997), 192.

[29] Ibid.

something uniquely about you or about me that no one else can or should say.

By focusing my attention on the preaching of my own conscience, Kierkegaard quite remarkably stops the argument about whether the preaching of repentance is efficacious, whether it is a good idea, whether "Sinners in the hands of an angry God" is a good sermon or not, by insisting that this kind of preaching is a game, is theater. The true preacher of repentance is already in you and is talking to you about yourself.

> He does not preach in any church or to an assembled crowd; he preaches in the secret recesses of the soul – and to you, whether you want to listen to him or not. He has nothing whatever to attend to than to you, and he sees to it that he is heard in the moment when everything around you is still, when the stillness makes you completely solitary.[30]

So solitude and stillness are absolutely essential for us to hear this preacher, which again means that we are not looking around at other people, but only at ourselves. And when we do enter into this stillness and this solitude, we enter into the experience that "God is." I love that phrase, "God is." "If you have never been solitary, then neither have you discovered that *God is*."[31] Only when we are silent, only when we are alone, only when we are accountable, and only when we are listening to the voice of conscience about ourselves, do we realize that God is. So the conscience is the God-relationship and our stillness and our silence are the experience and the awareness that God is, and that we are already in relationship to God.

This then raises the question, who is the God of conscience? Who is the God with whom I am already in relation? For Calvin, we are brought into relation with the judgment of God. For Kierkegaard, we are brought into relation with the omnipotent love of God the Creator. "What incomprehensible omnipotence of love! … This

---

[30] Ibid.   [31] Kierkegaard, *Works of Love*, 384.

omnipotence constrains itself (something more wonderful than the coming into existence of all creation!) and lovingly makes created being something in relation to itself – what wonderful omnipotence of love!"[32] God has such omnipotence of love that God can withdraw God's power out of love to create out of nothing a creature that can freely relate to God. God sets this creature free out of love. God creates out of nothing a creature who is free to relate to the love that is God. That is what it means to be an individual human being. In order for this to work, the power of God can never override my freedom, because the omnipotence of love creates me out of nothing into someone who is given the freedom to relate to the God who created me. For Kierkegaard the idea of *creatio ex nihilo* is individual. Each one of us is created out of nothing. Each one of us is created out of omnipotent love, and we are all summoned to relate to the one who created us out of love. So the voice of conscience is the voice of the love that created us. In a way, the voice of conscience is the voice of that love which springs up within us about which I spoke in the second chapter. There is a spring of love that wells up in every individual, and our conscience may well be the voice of that love. This is the love that created you. This is the love to which you already have a relationship. And the question becomes, how will we relate to this love?

According to Kierkegaard, the conscience tells us that the God who gives us everything also requires everything of us.[33] God gives us everything out of omnipotent love, but God thereby requires everything of us. This is where Kierkegaard thinks that human beings make a category mistake when they think about themselves and then when they think about God. If I as a human being require everything of you, you would experience that as a relationship of power, and you would be right. I can only obligate you in that way if I have power over you. For instance, the state has the power to obligate us because otherwise it will kill us, as we learn from Romans 13.

[32] Kierkegaard, *Christian Discourses*, 127.   [33] Ibid., 254.

We saw this clearly when the family would not return their son Elian Gonzalez to Cuba. The federal agents came in with their weapons at the ready and took him out of the closet in which he was being hidden. Many were shocked by this, but that is because they forgot that the power of the state comes ultimately from the fact that if you persist in defying it, it has the power to kill you. So human beings obligate each other by power. When we are humbled before others that is usually a situation of powerlessness on our part, over against the power of the other person. On the other hand, we understand love to be the remission of such an obligation, freeing us from such crushing power. However we cannot apply this model of power and love to God, for with God power and love are exactly the opposite of what they are for human beings. God's power could not possibly bring us under obligation to God, because for God's power we are nothing. How could you compare a human being to the Creator of the universe? But God's love is an entirely different thing. "But for God you are nothing, and therefore it is his love, just as it made you to be something, that requires something of you."[34] It was love that made us into something, and it is the love that obligates us, and obligates us entirely. The love that creates us claims the entirety of our lives, and it asks us if we will freely surrender our lives to God. Will you lose your life to me? Will you let it go? Will you surrender it? Will you sacrifice it to me out of love? I am love. I created you out of love. My love claims you now. Will you freely acknowledge that claim? This is the question our conscience is asking each one of us every single day. Will you let go?

The problem is, we do not. When we start to feel that claim of God's omnipotent love, and become more fully aware that God is, we start to sense that God does not just want a little bit of our lives, like an hour of worship on Sunday. God wants everything. The love that gave you everything wants everything from you. You had thought that by coming into relationship with the love of God, you

---

[34] Ibid., 127.

would be given comfort, that the requirement would be alleviated, only to discover to your dismay that it is precisely the love of God that claims the totality of your life. When you come into relationship with God, you realize the terror and the wonder that God will take everything, everything, everything, from us, but will do so in order to give everything to us. "This can be done only by God, who takes everything, everything, everything – in order to give everything – who does not piecemeal take little or much or exceedingly much but takes infinitely everything if you hold fast to him."[35] What God asks us to do is freely let go of the freedom we have been given to live independently of God, so that God can give us everything good in return. When we freely let go of the something we are, God gives us everything. The God who created us out of nothing asks us to give everything to God, so that God can give us Godself. And God does this precisely because God is Love.

This is terrifying to us because it means becoming nothing before God. "Therefore never hold fast to God … 'never hold fast to God, because by holding fast to him you lose what no one who holds fast to the world ever lost, not even the person who lost the most – you lose unconditionally everything.'"[36] The Love that is God asks us freely to become nothing before God, so that God can be everything in us. Moreover, in order to relate to God, we must deny the self-love of the alliance by which we try to make ourselves something, in order to enter into relation with the Love that is God. "What the world honors and loves under the name of love is an alliance in self-love … By love, however, God understands self-sacrificing love in the divine sense, the self-sacrificing love that sacrifices everything in order to make room for God."[37] Kierkegaard thinks that we are all dimly aware that this is the requirement, that this is the cost of coming into relation with the eternal love of God. It is terrifying to us, the way we can imagine coming into the sphere of gravity of a black hole would be for a star – you can almost hear it screaming for

[35] Kierkegaard, *Works of Love*, 103.   [36] Ibid.   [37] Ibid., 119.

its life. And so in order to escape the annihilating gravity of God's love, we get busy with what Kierkegaard thinks we call the real earnestness of life. We try to make something of ourselves. "Above all, be an earnest person by having forsaken the one and only earnestness, to relate yourself to God, to become nothing."[38] We can only do this if we stop relating to God, and start comparing ourselves to one another, for it is only in comparison with others that I can think that I am something. "Then one person compares himself with another, and the one who has understood somewhat more than others prides himself on being something."[39] My greatest anxiety would be that I would fail to make myself into something, that I would actually amount to nothing. "But to become a councilor of justice – to be that would be something, and he must above all become something in the world; to be nothing at all is something to despair over."[40] Imagine my despair if at my retirement dinner, those who knew me got up and said, "Randall was a nice person, I suppose, but he never really amounted to anything. He never made anything out of himself." We desperately want to be something, even if it is a janitor, even if it is a city counselor, let alone a professor of theology – we want to be something, and the only way to be something is in comparison to others. We must forget about God, and only pretend to relate to God, because we know that God will take all of this away. God will reveal that the human status and honor by which we made ourselves into something is actually despair. All of the "something" into which we seek to make ourselves is in truth so empty that if you really come to believe it, if you really buy into the status, if you really buy into the privilege, if you really buy into that being your identity, you are already dead, and people who look at you will see it. Your eyes will be hollow. There will be no life there. It is all despair, even if the world praises it for being the happiest of lives. But we cannot stop ourselves, we have to become something, because otherwise we will lose everything. The tragedy is that when we do try to become

[38] Ibid., 103.   [39] Ibid., 102.   [40] Kierkegaard, *Christian Discourses*, 44.

something, we really do lose everything, because we lose God. All this other stuff of human status and glory is nothing – it is the illusory fluff of nothingness, whereas God is everything.

So when God claims us in conscience, God claims everything. And if we stay in this relation long enough, the sense of annihilation will give rise to a deep sense of wonder. By becoming nothing before God, I become transparent to myself. By becoming nothing before God, I rest transparently in the power that established me. The love that I sense as a deep threat will give rise to awe, because when I begin to consent to this love which is taking everything away from me, when I start to let go, it gives me everything in return.

> He, the weak one, has totally given up this something into which love made him, has wholeheartedly consented to God's taking away all that could be taken. God is only waiting for him to give in love his humble, his glad consent and thereby to give it up completely, so that he is utterly weak – and then God is strongest.[41]

The love of God will give me everything, but only when I become nothing in relation to it. And I know I cannot stop the process in order once again to become something, for the more I freely become nothing before the love that is God, the more blessedness I feel, for "this annihilation before God is so blessed that you at every moment would seek to return to this annihilation more intensely, more warmly, more fervently than the blood returns to the place from which it was forcibly expelled."[42] By becoming nothing before God, you suddenly feel the love of God springing up more and more in yourself, making you into its instrument, so that this love can flow through you to your neighbor. However, this will only happen if you deny yourself, if you surrender yourself, if you let yourself be annihilated by the creative love of God; but when you do, you will be absolutely lost in wonder.

If, however, a person knew how to make himself truly what he is – nothing – and knew how to set the seal of patience on what he had

---

[41] Ibid., 128–29.   [42] Kierkegaard, *Works of Love*, 103.

understood – ah, then his life, whether he is the greatest or the lowest, would even today be a joyful surprise and be filled with blessed wonder and would be that throughout his days, because there is only one eternal object of wonder – that is God – and only one possible hindrance to wonder – and that is a person when he wants to be something.[43]

The love that is God brings a blessedness and a joy that you could never imagine, but in the midst of an annihilation that is terrifying. The love of God brings a comfort beyond words because the intimacy of this relationship with God goes far beyond anything we know in the human life, but it is deeply challenging because the claim of this love is absolute and total. This, by the way, is something that Kierkegaard learned from Judaism. Every action, every thought, every minute of your life is claimed by God. Christianity makes an even more radical claim, but we think we have escaped all obligation by believing that God is Love. So Kierkegaard always uses Judaism as a test case to see if Christians understand the claim of God's love, and he was convinced that we do not. "And now since people are so eager to be something, it is no wonder that however much they talk about God's love they are reluctant to become really involved with him, because his requirement and his criterion reduce them to nothing."[44] But when we do allow this claim of love to take us, when we freely surrender ourselves – not when it is taken from us, but when we consent to let it go – this is in fact human blessedness. "What is required of a human being is that he shall lose himself in wonder over God," that she shall lose herself in wonder over God. "The worshiper who has lost himself, and in such a way that this is the only thing he wishes to be rid of, has won God."[45]

[43] Søren Kierkegaard, *Eighteen Upbuilding Discourses*, ed. and trans. Howard V. Hong and Edna H. Hong (Princeton University Press, 1990), 225–26.
[44] Kierkegaard, *Works of Love*, 102.
[45] Kierkegaard, *Christian Discourses*, 130–31.

The obligation under which our conscience places us is not the obligation of judgment, but the obligation of love. The voice we hear in the stillness, in the solitude, in the silence, is the voice of this love. When we consent to this voice, and turn away from our busyness and our attempt to make ourselves something, we learn to our astonishment that becoming nothing before God expresses the truth of what it means to exist as a human creature in relation to God, and is the highest expression of human freedom. The one thing that keeps wonder out of our lives is our constant striving to be something, whereas our willingness to become nothing before God is the source of deep and never-ending wonder, for when you lose everything to God, you gain everything.

Then let the annihilation, the inner annihilation before God, have its terror, have its pain – the inspiring certainty ought to be the more blessed to a person. How terrible, how terrible, if a person, because for you his most honest striving is nothing, then took occasion to abandon himself to inactivity, or if he completely gave up wanting to be involved with you in order to become an earnest person who earnestly strives to become something in the world.[46]

---

[46] Søren Kierkegaard, *"For Self-Examination" and "Judge for Yourself,"* ed. and trans. Howard V. Hong and Edna H. Hong (Princeton University Press, 1990), 167.

6 | Hoping for all others, fearing for myself: John Calvin and Julian of Norwich

The subject of this chapter concerns the relationship between the wrath and love of God in the theology of John Calvin, brought into dialogue with Julian of Norwich. The title of this chapter, however, is inspired by a passage from Kierkegaard, although it seems to encapsulate my sense of Julian quite well. Kierkegaard expresses his inability to understand the thinking of those who are sufficiently assured of their own eternal salvation that they are led to worry about the salvation of others.

> They are sure enough about what will happen to them in that separation of eternity, are sure enough about the matter of their own salvation, that they are the righteous, or sure enough that they are believers – and now they raise the question whether others can be saved. For me the matter has never appeared that way; nothing has ever crossed my mind but that every other person would easily be saved; in *my* view it was doubtful only in regard to *me*. Yes, if I had caught myself doubting the salvation of anyone else at all, it would have been enough to make me despair of my own.[1]

It is ironic that I have chosen this theme, for my first work in the Reformation was about the assurance of faith, and in that model, you are most sure of your own election, you are most sure of God's love for you personally, individually. You are less sure of other members of the evangelical community, and are certain that most people

---

[1] *Christian Discourses*, 209–10.

both inside and outside of the church are eternally lost.[2] In my own thinking, as much as I love Calvin, this has become a highly problematic position. I think Christianity works best when we hope for all others and we fear only for ourselves, and what we ought to fear most in ourselves is our tendency to view others as being under divine judgment, while we personally are under mercy. So the theme for this chapter will focus especially on the relationship between the love and wrath, the mercy and the anger of God, both in John Calvin and in Julian of Norwich.

One of the central ways in which Calvin thinks about the love of God is by way of contrast. He has this aesthetic idea that you appreciate one reality in the best way by seeing it in light of the contrasting reality over against which it stands, and the primary contrasting reality by which we know the love of God, for Calvin, is the wrath of God. This wrath is actually quite pervasive throughout his theology. He says that after the fall of Adam and Eve into sin, "the Lord determined that his anger should like a deluge overflow all parts of the earth so that wherever we turn, we see that God is against us," that God is angry with us, that God is wrathful toward us, and this wrath awakens our own sense of sin and the fact that we have lost this relationship with God.[3] So even though the universe is the beautiful image of God about which I spoke in the first chapter, we also look about and see the divine curse, and this awakens our own sense of sinfulness, and it also makes us aware that we have included all other creatures in this corruption that we brought into the universe. I think it is quite remarkable that Calvin highlights this theme, that human sin corrupted non-human creation and brought suffering and death into that sphere as well. We are responsible for the suffering and death we see in other creatures. So Calvin accounts

[2] Randall C. Zachman, *The Assurance of Faith: Conscience in the Theology of Martin Luther and John Calvin* (Louisville, KY: Westminster John Knox Press, 2005).

[3] Comm. Genesis 3:17, CO 23:73A; CTS 1:173.

for the cruel and death-dealing aspects of our contemplation of the universe by claiming that God's anger, like a deluge, has overflowed the earth and the heavens themselves. This theme forms the transition in the *Institutes* from the knowledge of God the Creator to the knowledge of God the Redeemer.

> The natural order was that the frame of the universe should be the school in which we were to learn piety, and from it pass over to eternal life and perfect felicity. But after man's rebellion, our eyes – wherever they turn – encounter God's curse. This curse, while it seizes and envelops innocent creatures through our fault, must overwhelm our souls with despair.[4]

After Adam's fall into sin, we can only view the goodness of creation over against a horizon of wrath, which Calvin, like Irenaeus before him, sees spreading more and more in the Genesis narrative, as human sin becomes more and more pervasive.

Moreover, Calvin frames his whole discussion of the saving work of Christ by our own experience of God's wrath, by our own awareness of divine anger.

> No one can descend into himself and seriously consider what he is without feeling God's wrath and hostility toward him. Accordingly, he must anxiously seek ways and means to appease God – and this demands satisfaction. No common assurance is required, for God's wrath and curse always lie upon sinners until they are absolved of guilt. Since he is a righteous Judge, he does not allow his law to be broken without punishment, but is equipped to avenge it.[5]

We can see in this passage all of the themes related to the anger of God: God's hostility, wrath, curse, and vengeance. If we are rightly to appreciate what Christ has done for us, we must begin with our experience of divine anger against us and the threat of divine

---

[4] Inst. ii.vi.i, OS iii.320.13–18; LCC 341.
[5] Inst. ii.xvi.i, OS iii.483.5–12; LCC 504.

vengeance towards us. Without this sense of divine anger, we cannot appreciate what Christ has done for us. So the role of divine anger now becomes quite experiential. You descend into yourself, you see your own sin, and then you see the reason why God hates you, why God should act in vengeance against you, why God is angry with you.

Socinus posed a very acute question to Calvin with regard to this issue. Socinus pointed out that according to Scripture, Christ was sent to die because God already loved us. How then can Calvin claim that Christ's death appeases God's wrath, if Paul says that the death of Christ is the pledge of God's love for us (Romans 5:8)? Christ's death did not make it possible for God to love us; Christ died because God already loved us. Calvin defends his way of framing this position by claiming that without our experience of divine anger, we would not appreciate the love of God in Christ. Unless we experience God as against us, unless I experience God as against me, I cannot know the love of God for me in Jesus Christ.

> To sum up: since our hearts cannot, in God's mercy, either seize upon life ardently enough or accept it with the gratefulness we owe, unless our minds are first struck and overwhelmed by fear of God's wrath and by dread of eternal death, we are taught by Scripture to perceive that apart from Christ, God, is, so to speak, hostile to us, and his hand is armed for our destruction; to embrace his benevolence and fatherly love in Christ alone.[6]

Unless we see for ourselves that the hand of God is raised against us in anger to destroy us, we will not appreciate the love that God has for us in Christ. Thus the vengeance of God frames our appreciation of the love of God for sinners.

The wrath of God also plays a very prominent, and quite controversial, role in the suffering and death of Christ. My Roman Catholic brothers and sisters at Notre Dame find this position to be very

---

[6] Inst. II.xvi.2, OS III.484.11–18; LCC 505.

problematic theologically, since according to Thomas Aquinas there was not a moment in Christ's life or death when he did not experience the beatific vision. However, Calvin thinks that the Latin edition of the Apostle's Creed that says that Christ descended into Hell, and not just to the dead, is correct, and should be taught to all, even to children, and it therefore appears in his 1545 *Geneva Catechism*. Without this claim, Calvin was convinced that we will not understand how much it cost the Son of God to redeem us from the anger of God, from the curse of God, from the vengeance of God. Christ's descent to Hell, for Calvin, begins in the agony of Gethsemane. Calvin observes that Jesus could not be so anxious and terrified just by the spectacle of his own death, since there are philosophers, and even regular people, who have gone to their death far more courageously than Jesus does. Jesus is thrown to the ground by his anguish, and in one version of the Gospel of Luke, he is so terrified that he sweats blood. Calvin claims that he is not terrified of his own death, but rather of the vengeance of God which he is going to bring upon himself by substituting himself for us in our place as guilty sinners. Christ will experience in himself, in the depths of his soul, the righteous vengeance of God that should fall on us. "No – it was expedient at the same time for him to undergo the severity of God's vengeance, to appease his wrath and satisfy his just judgment."[7] This experience of wrath culminates with Christ's cry of dereliction, "My God, my God, why have you forsaken me?" Jesus feels as though God has plotted his own destruction, and this reveals to us that he suffers the death that God in his wrath inflicts on the wicked. "This is what we are saying: he bore the weight of divine severity, since he was 'stricken and afflicted' [cf. Is. 53:5] by God's hand, and experienced all the signs of a wrathful and avenging God."[8]

Even though Calvin paradoxically claims that Christ also experiences the love of God for him as God's beloved Son, his position

---

[7] Inst. II.xvi.10, OS III.495.5–7; LCC 515.
[8] Inst. II.xvi.11, OS II.496.21–23; LCC 517.

is quite different than that of Thomas Aquinas, and is abhorrent for much Roman Catholic Christology, in which Jesus experiences the beatific vision all through his life, death, burial, and resurrection. So this is a very strange claim for Calvin to make, and even the Lutherans were a little shaken by this claim. But Calvin is insistent that Christ experiences the weight of divine anger and all the signs of an angry and avenging God, for once we have experienced the weight of God's anger on us when we descend into ourselves, we must see it transferred to Christ, to the Son of God in Christ, or else we will be anxious ourselves, as though the just vengeance of God were still hanging over us. "We must, above all, remember this substitution, lest we tremble and remain anxious throughout life – as if God's righteous vengeance, which the Son of God has taken upon himself, still hung over us."[9] We have to transfer our sin and our guilt, and especially the anger and vengeance of God, from ourselves to Christ, or else our anxiety about God's anger and vengeance will never go away, and in a sense, you can detect in Calvin as in Luther an anxiety of conscience that never really does go away. They both have a deep sense of God's anger in their conscience that they have constantly to allay by appealing to Christ, by transferring that wrath and anger from themselves to Christ. So the anger of God plays an important and essential role in Calvin's understanding of creation, our subsequent need for Christ, and the work that Christ does on our behalf. We must appreciate how our sin brought God's anger and curse on all creation, and we must experience that wrath in our consciences, to appreciate the way Christ has taken that anger upon himself and freed us from it. We must constantly remember this substitution, so that when our conscience again senses that God might be angry with us, we in faith transfer that anger to Christ and then see God's love for us in Christ.

This, however, is not the end of the story. You not only need to experience wrath in yourself to appreciate what Christ has done for

9 Inst. II.xvi.5, OS III.489.16–20; LCC 510.

you; you also need to see the wrath of God on most of humanity in order to appreciate the electing love that God has personally for you. In other words, I must come to appreciate God's love for me by seeing for myself God's hatred of others. Calvin is convinced that you only truly appreciate how much God loves you when you see how much God hates others, how angry God is with others. "We shall never be clearly persuaded, as we ought to be, that our salvation flows from the wellspring of God's free mercy until we come to know his eternal election, which illuminates God's grace by this contrast: that he does not indiscriminately adopt all into the hope of salvation, but gives to some what he denies to others."[10] Once more we come to know the reality of God's grace and mercy by the contrast with God's anger and wrath, only now as directed towards the human race. We only know that the mercy of God is freely given if we know that it is given to some and denied to others, and this denial means that they are under the wrath and anger of God according to the eternal will of God. Thus, when Paul speaks of some being vessels of mercy while others are vessels of wrath (Romans 9:22–23), Calvin notes that "God is said to have ordained from eternity those whom he wills to embrace in love, and those upon whom he wills to vent his wrath."[11] According to Calvin's way of thinking, God not only needs to display God's wrath so that we can appreciate God's mercy, but God also needs to express both God's wrath and God's mercy on the human race, "since election itself could not stand except as set over against reprobation."[12] We therefore must know that others are under wrath, that others are under the anger and vengeance of God. We have to see it because this contrasting vision clarifies our appreciation of God's love for us.

The fulness of the divine mercy towards the elect is more clearly confirmed by this. The elect differ from the reprobate only in the fact of

---

[10] Inst. III.xxi.1, OS IV.369.10–14; LCC 921.

[11] Inst. III.xxiv.17, OS IV.430.4–5; LCC 985.

[12] Inst. III.xxiii.1, OS IV.394.2–3; LCC 947.

their deliverance from the same gulf of destruction. This, moreover, is by no merit of their own, but by the free goodness of God. It must, therefore, be true that the infinite mercy of God towards the elect will gain our increasing praise, when we see how wretched are all those who do not escape his wrath.[13]

We must see signs of the eternal wrath and anger of God on the reprobate in order to see fully the love of God for us. "For whoever are of the number of the reprobate, as they are vessels made for dishonor [cf. Rom. 9:21], so they do not cease by their continual crimes to arouse God's wrath against themselves, and to confirm by clear signs that God's judgment has already been pronounced upon them – no matter how much they vainly resist it."[14]

According to Calvin, even the fall in Adam into sin and death serves these contrasting destinies of humanity. Calvin asks, Why is it that all human beings fall into sin when Adam falls into sin? Human nature fell in Adam because of this one person's sin. Calvin knows that there is no necessity of this happening, and so God must have willed to set things up this way, so that due to the sin of Adam most human beings would eternally perish. "Again I ask: whence does it happen that Adam's fall irremediably involved so many peoples, together with their infant offspring, in eternal death unless it so pleased God?"[15] God willed before creation that most human beings would be vessels of God's wrath unto destruction, so that the elect would know just how much God loves them by this contrast. And this leads Calvin to conclude that God's relationship with most human beings is one of wrath, anger, and vengeance. "Whence it comes about that the whole world does not belong to its Creator except that grace rescues from God's curse and wrath and eternal death a limited number who would otherwise perish.

[13] Comm. Romans 9:23, CO 49:188; CNTC 8:211.
[14] Inst. III.xxiii.12, OS IV.406–7; LCC 961.
[15] Inst. III.xxiii.7, OS IV.401.25–27; LCC 955.

But the world itself is left to its own destruction, to which it has been destined."[16] That is a really remarkable sentence. If you wonder why Calvin has the reputation he does, you need look no further than quotes like that one. But this shows the degree to which Calvin frames his understanding of God's love by contrast with the pervasiveness of God's anger and wrath. Even if God loves you, this love is framed by the wrath you should first feel in your conscience. But now that you know and believe that God loves you, you must know that God hates others, and you must see God's hatred of others for yourself. You must see the difference between yourself and them, to know what it means for God to love you. Were someone to raise the objection on the basis of Scripture, that God hates nothing that God has made, Calvin maintains that this does not affect the doctrine he wishes to teach, for "the reprobate are hateful to God, and with very good reason. For, deprived of his Spirit, they can bring forth nothing but reason for cursing."[17] But of course Calvin knows that they are destitute of the Spirit because God refuses to give it to them. Thus God hates them because God wants to hate them. God creates them to fall into sin so that God can hate them, and carry out that hatred by destroying them. "Paul does not inform us that the ruin of the ungodly is foreseen by the Lord, but that it is ordained by his counsel and will. Solomon also teaches us that not only was the destruction of the godly foreknown, but the ungodly themselves have been created for the specific purpose of perishing (Prov. 16:4)."[18] You can see why Jerome Bolsec, a physician in Geneva in the 1550s, was horrified by this teaching, and created a major doctrinal conflagration in Geneva when he said that this doctrine makes God into an arbitrary tyrant, which resulted in his expulsion from the city. So Calvin maintained and defended this position throughout his life, in spite of opposition from friend and foe alike. The hatred of God for most of humanity

---

[16] Inst. III.xxii.7, OS IV.387.24–27; LCC 940.

[17] Inst. III.xxiv.17, OS IV.431.24–26; LCC 986–87.

[18] Comm. Romans 9:18, CO 49:184; CNTC 8:207–8.

is essential to Calvin's theology, and it is also essential that the elect see this hatred that God has for others, for otherwise they will never know what it means to be loved by God. Their own hope is predicated on the destruction of others, and they can see how much God loves them by comparing themselves with what happens to others.

One could make a compelling argument that Calvin derives his vision of this contrast between God's love and wrath from the Exodus, and develops this as his own paradigm. If Julian is correct, this may be one essential area in which Christianity moves away from the Exodus paradigm. In the Exodus, the Israelites come to know how much God loves them by the destruction of their enemies. One of the oldest confessions of faith in Scripture commemorates this contrast. "Sing to the Lord, for he has triumphed gloriously; horse and rider he has thrown into the sea" (Exodus 15:21). Israel knows the love of God because God saved them from affliction and destroyed before their eyes those who oppressed them. They were delivered through the sea and Pharaoh and his army were drowned. Calvin does in fact appeal to this contrast to note that "there was no difficulty in distinguishing between God's wrath and his fatherly love."[19] The Psalms themselves echo this exodus rhythm, for the Psalmist knows God's love by the fact that he is delivered while his enemy is destroyed. Calvin also has solid evidence from Scripture that this same dynamic is being exhibited in Christ and the preaching of the Gospel, supported in particular by Paul's teaching in Romans 9. This makes his position really quite tenacious in that regard.

Moreover, Calvin thinks that the contrast between the election of grace and rejection of wrath takes place predominantly by the preaching of the Word, making the Gospel itself an instrument of this contrasting response. He thinks that this is revealed in two ways: first, by the scope of the preaching of the Gospel, and second, by the mixed reception the Gospel receives where it is preached. "In actual fact, the covenant of life is not preached equally among

---

[19] Comm. Exodus 14:31, CO 24:115; CTS 3:253.

all men, and among those to whom it is preached, it does not gain the same acceptance either constantly or in equal degree. In this diversity the wonderful depth of God's judgment is made known."[20] God manifests the distinction between those whom God loves and those whom God hates by sending the Gospel to be preached in one nation or locale instead of another. This is already quite an alarming picture, for if you look at a map in Calvin's time, the Gospel as he understood it is not being preached in most of Europe. There is a remnant of the elect hidden in the Roman Church, but the Gospel is not being preached except in a very few isolated little points of light, such as Wittenberg, Strasbourg, Zurich, and Geneva. Thus the map of Europe already manifests the distinction between God's anger and God's love. If you think about this geographically, let alone demographically, the situation is quite alarming, for the scope of preaching is very narrow. And once people begin to realize that the world is so much larger than Calvin was aware, which begins to happen in the Enlightenment, many people cannot believe that the civilizations of China, India, Africa, and the Americas were created by God only to be eternally destroyed. All these civilizations, lasting thousands of years, had no meaning before God other than to destroy them? Calvin is not aware of this, but the Calvinist position comes in for some pretty heavy weather once people realize how narrow the preaching of the Gospel has been even geographically, although in Calvin's day the scope in Europe was already quite limited, as we have noted. We also need to keep in mind that Calvin thinks you can see the wrath of God manifested in the synagogues, owing to their tenacious rejection of the Gospel. Calvin thought that the Jews as a whole bore all the marks of divine reprobation, even though there are elect Jews hidden in their midst. And they can manifest these signs of reprobation even in the way they interpret a verse of Scripture, for instance when God is said to rest on the seventh day.

[20] Inst. III.xxi.1, OS IV.368.33–38; LCC 920–21.

Here the Jews, in their usual method, foolishly trifle, saying, that God being anticipated in his work by the last evening, left certain animals imperfect, of which kind are fauns and satyrs, as though he had been one of the ordinary artificers who have need of time. Ravings so monstrous prove the authors of them to have been delivered over to a reprobate mind, as a dreadful example of the wrath of God.[21]

But even where the Gospel is preached, it is not received in the same way, and this also manifests the grace and wrath of God. Paul himself notes that God works both life and death through the preaching of the Gospel, and Calvin takes this to mean that the acceptance and rejection of the Gospel manifest to us the eternal love and hatred of God. Calvin claims that there is daily evidence of this distinction that anyone can see. "If the same sermon is preached, say, to a hundred people, twenty receive it with the ready obedience of faith, while the rest hold it valueless, or laugh, or hiss, or loathe it."[22] One can imagine Calvin standing high up in the pulpit of St. Pierre in Geneva and looking out to observe how people are responding to his sermons. We know from biographers that members of the congregation would frequently jeer at Calvin, and would play skittles during the sermon, or even fart in his direction while he preached.[23] They also made up jingles to the psalm tunes he had them sing, often in mockery of Calvin himself, and sarcastically dismissed the doctrine of "fucking predestination."[24] So it was not a pretty picture that he saw when he looked down at the congregation, and you can imagine that in his mind, he is thinking:

> Go ahead and laugh now, keep it up, because I can already see by your laughter that God eternally hates you, and will destroy you under his wrath and vengeance. I will comfort myself with this realization. So

---

[21] Comm. Genesis 2:3, CO 23:34A; CTS 1:107.

[22] Inst. III.xxiv.12, OS IV.424.8–10; LCC 979.

[23] Bernard Cottret, *Calvin: A Biography*, trans. M. Wallace McDonald (Grand Rapids, MI: William B. Eerdmans Publishing Company, 2000), 250–51.

[24] Ibid., 211.

make fun of the Gospel all you like – your mockery reveals all the more clearly to those of us who hear with pious docility how much God loves us, in contrast to how much God hates you.

Can you imagine preaching and looking out at your congregation and thinking of these things in your heart? So not even the preaching of the Gospel can reveal God's love without also revealing God's wrath, and you can see both of these manifesting themselves in each congregation.

The contrast between divine love and hatred also has a rather stark effect on the way Calvin himself teaches, which is something of which we need to be aware when we read him. Calvin distinguishes between those of his readers who are docile, obedient and teachable, and those who are resistant, contentious and argumentative. He teaches the former gently, leading them by the hand as a guide to the right knowledge of God and themselves, and his prose is really quite remarkable, making him one of the finest theological writers in the Christian tradition. But he is certain that this is not his only task. He is called not only to lead the teachable by the hand, but also to strive in hand-to-hand combat with the contentious and the obstinate. "Hitherto it has been my particular intention to lead by the hand those who are teachable, but not to strive hand to hand with the inflexible and the contentious. But now the truth which has been peaceably shown must be maintained against all the calumnies of the wicked."[25] Since God providentially leads the docile while also striving in anger with those who resist God's governance, Calvin also is going to oppose in anger those who resist his teaching, since God is also angry with them. So Calvin clearly and intentionally mirrors the distinction between God's mercy and God's vengeance in his method of teaching. Philipp Melanchthon, one of the consummate teachers of the Christian tradition and certainly of the Reformation period, pleaded with Calvin to teach only

---

[25] Inst. I.xiii.21, OS III.136.3–7; LCC 145–46.

in the first way, by peaceably and clearly setting forth the truth, for he thought that the church had been ruined by the contentiousness of the scholastics. So he pleaded with Calvin to limit himself only to teaching calmly, placidly and clearly, leaving the rest to take care of itself. But Calvin rejected these pleas from Melanchthon, insisting instead that teaching the Gospel is just like rebuilding the walls of Jerusalem. You need a trowel in one hand and a sword in the other, to build up the godly and fight off the ungodly.

You see this same distinction in the language Calvin uses with those who oppose him, with those who contend with him. He rarely refers to them as human beings, and if he does, he describes them as delirious and insane lunatics, and their positions as "perverse ravings."[26] But his preferred method is to describe them as animals or even monsters. So Servetus is a "frenzied person," but from his morass "another similar monster has come forth."[27] Lucretius is a "filthy dog," and the Epicureans are a "pigsty."[28] Those who oppose Calvin's teaching on predestination are "venomous dogs" who "spew out more than one kind of venom against God."[29] Francis Higman has written a book on Calvin's style in his French theological treatises in which he notes this tendency in Calvin, but it is the same style that he uses in his Latin treatises.[30] He will describe his opponents as aping monkeys, or as pigs or dogs who vomit forth their madness. I think that reading this kind of language has an effect on the reader. One of the questions that has been posed during the celebration of Calvin's birth is why the Reformed tradition is the most fractious and divisive among all Christian traditions. It is hard to lay all of the blame for this on Calvin, but his vicious and dehumanizing rhetoric cannot have helped. My advisor, Brian

---

[26] Inst. I.xiii.21, OS III.136.3–7; LCC 145–46.

[27] Inst. I.xiii.22–23, OS III.137, 139; LCC 147, 149.

[28] Inst. I.v.5, OS III.48, 50; LCC 56, 58.

[29] Inst. III.xxiii.2, OS IV.395.21–22; LCC 949.

[30] Francis Higman, *The Style of John Calvin in his French Polemical Treatises* (London: Oxford University Press, 1967).

A. Gerrish, agrees with Melanchthon, that the harsh and extensive polemics in the *Institutes* interferes with the clarity of Calvin's order of teaching, which becomes clear when you only read the passages of docile clarity and skip the contentious sections. But Calvin thought that one could not be a teacher and fail to manifest anger for one's opponents even as one shows mercy towards one's teachable students. After all, by so doing the teacher is only mirroring the method used by God, for God gently leads the pious and angrily contends with the wicked.

This contrast also impacts a theme we have previously discussed, namely the commandment that we love our enemies, bless those who curse us, and pray for those who persecute us. Calvin acknowledges that Jesus wants us to set aside every thought of revenge, and to manifest the love we have for others by blessing our enemies. In the meantime, Calvin encourages us not to fail to commit our cause to God until he takes vengeance on the reprobate. In other words, we hope that our enemies will eventually come to their right mind and join us by professing faith in the same Gospel with us. But if they remain opposed to us, we take comfort in the fact that God will exercise vengeance on them on our behalf, to show that God cares for us and has wrath on them. Thus, in the midst of his discussion of the importance of blessing our enemies, Calvin assures the godly that "they have this comfort to lighten all their pains, that they do not doubt, that God will be the Avenger of determined malice, that he may show that he has had a care for the innocent."[31] It might strike us as a paradoxical attitude to have; that I love and bless my enemies even as I simultaneously look forward to the day when God will destroy them in vengeance, to show me how much God cares for me. But this for Calvin is one of the essential ways in which the godly can find comfort when they are being tormented by their ungodly persecutors. This was a huge pastoral issue in France during Calvin's time. The forces against the little communities of faith

---

[31] Comm. Matthew 5:45, CO 45:188; CNTC 1:198.

in France were very powerful and very strong, and Calvin's followers experienced extraordinary persecution, arrest, torture, and execution. Calvin could not bear to watch this happen without seeking comfort in the thought that those who afflict us now will be afflicted by Christ himself when he returns.

> But those impious ones who have flourished on earth he will cast into utter disgrace; he will turn their delights into tortures, their laughter and mirth into weeping and gnashing of teeth; he will trouble their peace with dire torment of conscience; he will punish their wantonness with unquenchable fire; he will also make them bow their heads in subjection to the godly, whose patience they have abused. For, as Paul testifies, this is righteousness, to repay with affliction the wicked who afflict the godly, when the Lord is revealed from heaven [2 Thess. 1:6–7]. This is our sole comfort. If it be taken away, either our minds must become despondent, or, to our destruction, be captivated with the empty solace of this world.[32]

If we cannot hope that God will have vengeance on our enemies, and eternally torture those who torture us now, then we can have no comfort in our persecution. So we bless our enemies, knowing that God will curse them, and we love them, looking forward to the day when they will fully experience just how intensely God hates them.

Not surprisingly, therefore, Calvin concludes his discussion of the knowledge of God the Redeemer with a vivid and imaginative description of the anger that God will show for all of eternity toward those whom God hates. "Now, because no description can deal adequately with the gravity of God's vengeance against the wicked, their torments and tortures are figuratively expressed to us by physical things, that is, by darkness, weeping, and gnashing of teeth, unquenchable fire, an undying worm gnawing at the heart."[33] Calvin wants his readers to appreciate the full gravity of divine vengeance

---

[32] Inst. III.ix.6, OS IV.176.27–38; LCC 718–19.
[33] Inst. III.xxv.12, OS IV.455.29–34; LCC 1007.

that will be shown to the reprobate, and so he exhorts his readers to imagine how dreadful it would be to experience God's hatred for eternity.

> For first, his displeasure is like a raging fire, devouring and engulfing everything it touches. Secondly, all creatures so serve him in the execution of his judgment that they to whom the Lord will openly show his wrath will feel heaven, earth, sea, living beings, and all that exists aflame, as it were, with divine anger against them, and armed to destroy them.[34]

Moreover, the reprobate will personally experience the anger of God toward them, for God will destroy them with no means of escape.

> Consequently, unhappy consciences will find no rest from being troubled and tossed by a terrible whirlwind, from feeling that they are being torn asunder by a hostile Deity, pierced and lanced by deadly darts, quaking at God's lightning bolt, and being crushed by the weight of his hand – so that it would be more bearable to go down into any bottomless depths and chasms than to stand for a moment in these terrors. What and how great is this, to be eternally and unceasingly besieged by God?[35]

This is the last scene we are to contemplate, in contrast to the eternal happiness of the godly in their union with God, before turning to the discussion of the church. This is how important it is to Calvin for the godly to meditate on the future vengeance that God will unleash on his enemies. Comfort yourself with this picture when they persecute you, and then by all means love, bless, and pray for them.

I would now like to turn to a figure who lived in Norwich, England, two centuries before Calvin, a woman named Julian. Julian was of unknown age, probably in her early thirties, and was living at home, probably unmarried, when she and all others around her thought

---

[34] Inst. III.xxv.12, OS IV.456.6–11; LCC 1008.
[35] Inst. III.xxv.12, OS IV.456.18–24; LCC 1008.

she was dying. The custom of the time – one of which Calvin, along with Karlstadt, was highly critical – was to place a crucifix before the dying person to comfort her, so that she could look on the cross of Christ and see her suffering as part of Christ's suffering, in order to be comforted in her hour of death. The thought was that even though the dying cannot speak, and might not be able to hear, they can still see, so if they can see the cross, it will bring them comfort. The priest comes as Julian thinks she is dying, props her up, and places the cross in front of her. She was in fact conscious during this time, and, realizing that the hour of death is also the Day of Judgment, she thinks, "For me today is the Day of Judgment." And of course the Day of Judgment is also the day of wrath, which is important to remember as we consider what was shown to her during this time. As she lies there contemplating the cross on her day of judgment, Christ appears to her throughout the day in various ways: sometimes physically, sometimes spiritually, sometimes verbally, and sometimes visually and verbally. Once she has had time to think and pray about the showings, she writes them down in a shorter and longer version.

One of the most remarkable things Julian sees as she lies there dying is that there is no anger in God, "for I saw quite clearly that where our Lord appears, everything is peaceful and there is no place for anger; for I saw no kind of anger in God, neither for a short time nor for a long one."[36] She is looking for God's anger, since it is her day of judgment, and Holy Church has told her that God is angry with sinners, and remains angry with them until they repent. The mercy of God then brings about the remission of the anger of God, which sounds just like Calvin's position on the subject. "From what I had already learned, I understood that the mercy of God would be the remission of [God's] anger after our time of sin," and so "therefore I took it that the remission of his anger would be one of

---

[36] Julian of Norwich, *Revelations of Divine Love*, trans. Elizabeth Spearing (London: Penguin Books, 1998), 112.

the principal points of [God's] mercy."[37] Moreover, she learns from the Word of God that one of the points of the faith to which she holds is that many shall be damned, which again sounds similar to Calvin. Among the damned are the angels who fell from heaven and became fiends, some of whom actually attack her during this time; people outside of Holy Church who were never baptized, such as the heathens and others; and those who have been baptized but live unrepentant lives. God's Word and Holy Church have taught her that all these are going to be damned and condemned to everlasting Hell, and this is what Julian also believes.[38] So as Christ is revealing himself to her, Julian asks him to show her Hell. She sees nothing.[39] This is quite unusual, and caught Julian completely off guard, for the fourteenth and fifteenth centuries created incredibly vivid portrayals of Hell, as one sees in Dante's *Divine Comedy*. But Juian sees nothing. She also looks for blame in God, as God must blame sinners, but she sees no blame in God. She looks for anger against sin, but sees no anger. She looks for damnation, and is shown nothing of damnation. All of this is utterly puzzling to her. And the remarkable thing about Julian is that throughout all of this she never let go of her faith in what the Church taught and what the Word of God also taught. But she also held to what God was showing her, that there is no anger in God, no wrath, no severity, no vengeance, and therefore no Hell.

She therefore learns to distinguish between two kinds of judgment. One kind of judgment assigns no blame and has no anger, and that is God's judgment. The other kind of judgment assigns blame and experiences anger, and that is human judgment.

> And according to this judgment it seemed to me that I had to acknowledge myself a sinner, and by the same judgment I understood that sinners deserve blame and anger one day; and I could see no blame and anger in God, and then I felt a longing greater than I can or may tell; for God himself revealed the higher judgment at the same time,

---

[37] Ibid., 109.   [38] Ibid., 86.   [39] Ibid., 87.

and therefore I was bound to accept it; and the lower judgment had been taught me before by Holy Church, and therefore I could in no way abandon the lower judgment.[40]

She does not abandon the higher judgment for the sake of the lower, nor the lower for the sake of the higher, but holds both of them together, creating in a sense an unresolved dialectic, which is why I chose to bring her into conversation with Calvin. She would not deny Calvin's contention that there is judgment and blame and anger for sin, but she would simply point him to a higher judgment than that, in which there is no judgment or anger or blame in God, nor could there possibly be, for God is love. "The first judgment, from God's righteousness, comes from his exalted, everlasting love, and this is the kind and lovely judgment which was shown throughout the previous revelation in which I saw him assign us no kind of blame."[41]

So Julian holds to both the higher and the lower judgment, but she is really intrigued by the former. She is deeply interested in why she sees no anger in God. She finally comes to see that "God is the goodness that cannot be angry, for he is nothing but goodness."[42] Anger is the opposite of goodness, and so it is ontologically impossible for God to be angry. Moreover, the only anger that Julian saw was human, and she also saw that God forgives us for that anger. "For the only anger I saw was man's, and he forgives us for that; for anger is nothing but contrariness and antagonism to peace and love, and it comes from lack of strength, or from lack of wisdom, or from lack of goodness – and it is not God who lacks these things but we who lack them."[43] The only anger she saw was human, and God forgives us for that. The reason we need forgiveness is that we are angry, which leads us into conflict with God and one another. God forgives our anger, and will not get angry at our sin in response. Moreover, anger on our part is not a sign of strength but of great weakness, whereas God's inability to be angry is not a sign of weakness but of God's

[40] Ibid., 106.   [41] Ibid.   [42] Ibid., 108.   [43] Ibid., 110.

power. We can see this in our own lives. Have you ever noticed that when you are losing an argument you get angry? We think that the anger will make up for the fact that we do not have a very good argument, that our position is weak. I think that is what Julian means. Anger reveals a deficit, a lack of wisdom, a lack of strength, a lack of goodness, and it is not God who lacks these things, but we who lack them. So God is ontologically incapable of anger, because anger is a deficit, a loss of peace, a loss of unity.

When Julian comes to see all of this, she has to admit "that the effect of God's mercy and forgiveness is to lessen and wear away our anger."[44] God has mercy on us and forgives us to wear out our anger, to just bleed it out of us, to take it away, to wear it away. My wife was telling me that she has read that our anger should be like ice, not like a rock. A rock, when you pour water on it, will not melt, but anger that is ice will melt when the love of God is poured on it, and that is what the mercy and forgiveness of God are meant to do. The mercy of God is not the remission of God's anger, but rather the removal of our anger. We know that we are in a right relationship to God when our anger is worn away, when we are made gentle, when we are made patient, when we are made more loving, when we are made more compassionate.

> It is the greatest impossibility conceivable that God should be angry, for anger and friendship are two contraries. It must needs be that the one who wears away and extinguishes our anger and makes us gentle and kind is himself always consistently loving and kind, which is the contrary of anger, for I saw quite clearly that where our Lord appears, everything is peaceful and there is no place for anger, for I saw no kind of anger in God.[45]

Julian conveys the lack of anger in God even in the way that she writes. She is mystified but she never gets upset. She is puzzled, but she patiently just tries to think these things through, even though

---

[44] Ibid., 111.   [45] Ibid., 112.

what God is showing her appears to contradict everything she has hitherto believed. What she sees in God is expressed in the tone of her writing, making her a model of theological language.

But if there is no anger in God, then why do we think that there is? Julian accounts for this on the basis of our own passionate response to the revelation of our sin. She does not try to explain away our experience of what we take to be divine anger; she rather accounts for it on the basis of our own sense of our sinfulness. She thinks that when God secretly touches our inner heart, and gently touches it with God's love – note that God does not terrify the sinner in anger, but gently touches the secret part of our soul with love – it reveals our sin, which awakens our sense of shame and fear. Once this gentle love reveals our sin and we see how filthy we are, and we clearly perceive the wrong we have done that we can never undo, then we are convinced God is angry with us, and we are convinced that we must do something in response. We must repent and turn again, so that God may have mercy on us and forgive us, and our conscience may find peace. Far from saying that this experience of sin is an illusion, she says, "And it is true."[46] Our experience of wrath is real, our sense that God must be angry with us is real, but Julian will not let us project this sense of wrath and anger into God. Just because you think God is angry does not mean that God is truly angry. On the contrary, were God truly to be angry with us as sinners, then all hope would be lost, for we would be destroyed. "Indeed, it seems to me that if God could be even slightly angry we could never have any life or place or being."[47] So if God is truly angry when you think God is angry, all hope is lost. If you even think that there is any vengeance in God at all, it is over because to you there would never be anything but vengeance. Your sin will convince you that God must hate you, and your conscience will tell you that God is angry with you, but you must not believe that this is true, because true divine anger would destroy us.

[46] Ibid., 97.   [47] Ibid., 112.

We must therefore learn the art of accusing ourselves properly without losing sight of the love that is God. God does want us to accuse ourselves, but God does not want us to believe that God accuses us. Hence we should accuse ourselves even as we believe that while we do so God is excusing us.

> And the way our Lord wants us to accuse ourselves is this: earnestly and truly seeing and recognizing our fall and the troubles that come from it, seeing and knowing that we can never make it good, but at the same time we should earnestly and truly see and know the everlasting love which he has for us, and his abundant mercy. And seeing and knowing this together in this way is the humble self-accusation which our Lord asks of us, and where it exists, he himself has brought it about.[48]

We should therefore work through our sense that God is angry with us until we become aware of the love of God that was always there, and that never changes. When we finally discover God's everlasting love, it feels like a new thing, as though God had changed God's attitude, and had remitted anger in mercy, but it is actually our penetration beyond what our sin is telling us to what has been true of God all along. It was love that revealed to us that we were sinners. It was love that made us think that God was angry with us. It was love that got us to see that God is not angry with us. And then our experience of being forgiven by a God who was never angry wears our anger away. It makes us more gentle, it makes us more loving, and it makes us more peaceful. For we come to see the love of God that can never be angry.

> For this is what was shown: that our life is all rooted and grounded in love, and without love we cannot live; and therefore to the soul which through God's special grace sees so much of his great and marvelous goodness, and sees that we are joined to him in love forever, it is the greatest impossibility conceivable that God should be angry.[49]

[48] Ibid., 127. [49] Ibid., 112.

The other thing of which Julian becomes aware is that what harms us the most is paying attention to the sins of others. When the love of God reveals sin to us, we realize that sin itself is the greatest suffering there is, for sin contradicts the love that is God. "Sin is much more vile and painful than hell."[50] Since the suffering of sin is greater than the pains of hell, you would never want to probe into the sins of your neighbor. You would not even want to see your neighbor's sin. If you did happen to see it, you should pray to God to take it away from your sight. And if God will not take it away from your sight, pray to God to give you a spirit of compassion, and pray to God to have mercy on that person. But above all, do not attend to the sins of others. It clouds your soul. It gets in the way.

> The soul that wants to be at peace must flee from thoughts of other people's sins as though from the pains of hell, begging God for a remedy and a help against it; for the consideration of other people's sins makes a sort of thick mist before the eyes of the soul, and during such times we cannot see the beauty of God unless we regard the sins with sorrow for those who commit them, with compassion and with a holy wish for God to help them.[51]

Our surprising realization that there is no anger or blame or vengeance in God must be reflected in our refusal to be interested in the sins of others, as well as our refusal to console ourselves with the thought that God is angry with others. Even though Holy Church teaches Julian that God will be eternally angry with many, she also sees that there is no anger in God, and she holds these two things together.

Julian also sees that since our sin creates tremendous evil within us and great suffering within us, God is the one who takes evil and turns it into good. This is God's nature. God takes any evil, even the greatest evil, and turns it into good. That is what God does. On the other hand, if there were anger in God, if there were vengeance in

---

[50] Ibid., 146.   [51] Ibid., 166.

God, God would repay evil with evil, and that is, by nature, impossible to God. God is the one who turns evil into good. Even though Julian does not mention this, I am reminded of what happens to Joseph in Genesis. God does not come down and take vengeance on his brothers for all of the evil they brought upon him; God quietly takes all the evil that the brothers intended against Joseph and uses it for good. That is Julian's understanding of God. That is what God always does. After all, God took the greatest evil, which is what Adam did, and turned it into the greatest good, which is what Christ did, thereby revealing the very nature of God. "So what our blessed Lord's teaching means is that we should take heed of the following: 'Since I have turned the greatest possible harm into good, it is my will that you should know from this that I shall turn all lesser evil into good.'"[52] This means that God is incapable to rendering evil for evil, which is what anger and vengeance do. God always works the greatest good out of the greatest evil, for this is what love does.

In terms of our own situation, the revelations of Julian are both comforting to us and challenging to us. Insofar as we are united more and more to God, we are made more gentle, we are made more peaceful, and we are made more loving and compassionate. However, insofar as we are still angry and judgmental, and still contemplate the sins of others and the anger God must have for them, we are in great danger, for we are separating ourselves from the love that is God. What jeopardizes our salvation, what jeopardizes our experience of God's love, is our refusal to stop being angry, our refusal to stop judging others, and our refusal to stop contradicting the nature of God. Insofar as we keep contradicting God by our anger and lack of compassion, we are in the greatest jeopardy. God is trying to make us safe, but we endanger ourselves by our own judgmental attitude and by our own anger, for "we are not blessedly safe in the possession of our eternal joy until we are in a state of peace and love."[53] This is why I would say in Julian's mind, we should, in

[52] Ibid., 82.   [53] Ibid., 113.

176

fact, hope for all others, and we should not even try to see their sin. But we should fear for ourselves precisely when we are angry, precisely when we are contrary and judgmental, for this keeps us from being united to God in love.

But even then, in spite of the danger to which we constantly expose ourselves, in spite of the sin of the world inside and outside of the Church, let alone in Julian herself, God famously tells her, "'It is true that sin is the cause of all this suffering, but all shall be well, and all shall be well, and all manner of things shall be well.'"[54] God tells her, yes, I know what the Church tells you, that there will be a time of wrath and vengeance, but I am telling you that on the last day that I am going to do a mighty work and all shall be well, and all manner of thing shall be well. And Julian is absolutely perplexed by this vision. She cannot figure this out, because she will not let go of the teaching of Holy Church, but she is also being told something by God to which she also must hold. She finally brings her concerns to God to try to find some kind of resolution.

> Holy Church teaches me to believe that all these shall be condemned to everlasting hell. And given all this, I thought it impossible that all manner of things should be well, as our Lord revealed at this time. And I received no other answer in showing from our Lord God but this: "What is impossible to you is not impossible to me. I shall keep my word and I shall make all things well."[55]

What seems impossible to Holy Church, what seems impossible to Julian and to us, that God would not have vengeance on those who oppose God, is not in fact impossible to God. It seems to me our own limitations and the limitations of Holy Church are rooted in an understandable and almost inevitable need to project our anger against our own sin and the sin of others into God. But when we do that, there is no freeing ourselves from anger, because we now have a divine validation of anger. We then think, well if God is angry,

54 Ibid., 80.   55 Ibid., 86.

then I can be angry. And by so doing I would be in good company. After all, Jesus got angry, Jeremiah got angry, John the Baptist got angry, and so, by God, I am angry! That is actually Calvin's response to Melanchthon. The prophets got angry, Jesus got angry, so I as a teacher get angry. But God shows Julian that this way of thinking does not reflect the nature of God, and thus will not free us from the anger that is destroying us. We cannot imagine a life in which we are not angry with those who harm us, and we cannot free ourselves from the temptation to comfort ourselves by fantasizing about the vengeance God will have on our enemies. But God shows Julian, and shows all of us, that what is impossible for us is not impossible for God.

Julian puzzled over this showing for most of the rest of her life. She became an anchoress at St. Julian's Church in Norwich, living in a cell behind the sanctuary, which was unfortunately destroyed in the Reformation, likely by followers of John Calvin. And she spent her years in solitude, giving spiritual guidance to the occasional visitor, and praying over the meaning of these showings, trying to understand what God meant by revealing this to her. And she finally got her answer, many years later.

> From the time that this was shown, I often longed to know what our Lord meant. And 15 years and more later, my spiritual understanding received an answer, which was this, "Do you want to know what your Lord meant? Know well that love was what he meant. Who showed this to you? Love. What did he show? Love. Why did he show it to you? For love. Hold fast to this and you will know and understand more of the same, but you will never understand or know from it anything else for all eternity."[56]

---

[56] Ibid., 179.

Conclusion

Our reconsideration of John Calvin has left us with many trajectories into the future, and I would like to take the remaining chapter to trace out where I see each trajectory heading, and also to answer questions that each trajectory raises for us.

First of all, Calvin himself would expand the scope of our contemplation of the universe to include not only the heavens beyond the earth, but also the works of God that confront us on earth. Calvin thought that the best place to proceed after contemplating the stars, planets, sun and moon was the atmosphere, for the sudden changes one sees there are a striking contrast to the abiding order, harmony, and symmetry one sees in the heavens, and thus provide a more striking testimony to the powers of God. Once again, this contemplation has one level for the unlearned, and another for the learned; but the investigations of the learned do not mean that the unlearned cannot profit from this contemplation, any more than the contemplation of the unlearned necessitates the rejection of more learned investigations. As we saw with regard to astronomy, the purpose of the learned investigation of the atmosphere would be to learn the natural causes of the natural effects we see, while simultaneously seeing all natural causes and effects as works of God that reveal the powers of God. Calvin was increasingly concerned that the method of Aristotle would raise the possibility that the mediate causes of atmospheric effects would blind the learned to the awareness that all such causes and effects are also the work of God.

Philosophers think not that they have reasoned skillfully enough about inferior causes, unless they separate God very far from his works. It is a diabolical science, however, which fixes our contemplations on the works of nature, and turns them away from God. If anyone who wished to know a man should take no notice of his face, but should fix his eyes only on the points of his nails, his folly might justly be derided. But far greater is the folly of those philosophers, who, out of mediate and proximate causes, weave themselves veils, lest they should be compelled to acknowledge the hand of God, which manifestly displays itself in his works.[1]

However, Calvin does not think that we arrive at this awareness by breaking the causal nexus with allegedly divine works, but rather by means of the experience of awe, astonishment, and wonder, which opens us up to the presence of God hidden within the events we seek to understand.

Once we have considered the marvels of the atmosphere, we should descend to contemplate the emergence of dry land from the water. According to the physics that Calvin knew, water is lighter than the earth, and hence has a natural tendency to cover the earth. Thus the emergence of dry land is a perpetual monument to the providential care of God for all life that lives on earth.

Natural philosophers confess, and experience openly proclaims, that the waters occupy a higher place than the earth. How is it then that, as they are fluid and naturally disposed to flow, they do not spread abroad and cover the earth, and how is it that the earth, which is lower in position, remains dry? In this we certainly perceive that God, who is ever attentive to the welfare of the human race, has inclosed the waters within certain invisible barriers, and keeps them shut up to this day.[2]

Our understanding of the emergence of dry land from the waters may be quite different than that of Calvin, but we can be no less

---

[1] Comm. Psalm 29:5, CO 31:289A; CTS 8:479.
[2] Comm. Psalm 33:7, CO 31:328A; CTS 8:544.

astonished that we have found a place to live on the surface of the earth, given the massive forces now known to us by plate tectonics. Indeed, we now know why life on the surface of the earth is even more fragile than Calvin thought, as we learn every time a volcano erupts or an earthquake levels a country, or unleashes a tsunami of devastating force and power. Following the lead of Calvin in our own day, and heeding his advice not to see Scripture as teaching us science, we can now marvel at the overwhelming forces at work in the dry land beneath us, and be grateful that we have been provided the space to live.

Calvin would then have us move on to the consideration of all of the abundant forms of life we encounter, especially in those regions that are furthest from human contact, interaction, and interest. We cannot but marvel when we see life flourishing in regions of the world human beings would find uninhabitable, especially in the wilderness. "Rivers run even through great and desolate wildernesses, where the wild beasts enjoy some blessing of God; and no country is so barren as not to have trees growing here and there, on which birds make the air to resound with the melody of their singing."[3] If we believe that God creates and cares for all that God has made, then we must contemplate with wonder the astonishing creatures with whom we share our planet. We now have a much greater sense of the diversity of life on earth than did Calvin, and also know that there have been many different periods of life on earth over the past billions of years, and we can now contemplate with astonishment the fossil records of those creatures that have come before us, whose presence then makes possible our presence here and now. Calvin also encourages us to consider and attend to the ways in which God provides food and habitat for all creatures, even the wild birds in the wilderness.

The Psalmist again treats of God's general providence in cherishing all the parts of the world. In the first place, he asserts, that by the

[3] Comm. Psalm 104:10, CO 32:89A; CTS 11:154.

watering of which he had spoken the trees are satiated, or filled with sap, that thus flourishing they may be a place of abode to the birds. He next declares, that the wild deer and conies have also their places of shelter, to show that no part of the world is forgotten by Him, who is the best of fathers, and that no creature is excluded from his care.[4]

Indeed, he considered it just as miraculous that God provides water for creatures in the mountains, as it is that God creates dry land for all creatures to inhabit.

Although it is necessary for the earth to be dry, to render it a fit habitation for us, yet, unless we had water to drink, and unless the earth opened her veins, all kinds of living creatures would perish. The prophet, therefore, speaks in commendation of that arrangement by which the earth, though dry, yet supplies us with water by its moisture.[5]

He also wants us to consider the ways in which these creatures of themselves add to the beauty of the world, apart from any consideration of their benefit for human life. God's care for the creatures of the deep, and the creatures of the wilderness, including far off places about which Calvin could not even imagine, should be the object of ceaseless contemplation and study, and cannot but heighten the wonder we experience in our world.

Finally, we should consider our own emergence into life, and the way we were delivered into this world and cared for when we emerged from our mother's womb. Calvin thinks that the birth of a single child should ravish us with astonishment and leave us speechless with wonder, were it not for the fact that the frequency of its occurrence blinds our eyes to its astonishing nature. Calvin thought that the fetus was imprisoned in a watery tomb, fouled by its own digestive waste, preserved by God's power until it emerged from the womb as from a grave:

[4] Comm. Psalm 104:16, CO 32:91–92; CTS 11:160.
[5] Comm. Psalm 104:10, CO 32:88C; CTS 11:153.

have we not equal reason to marvel that the infant, shut up within its mother's womb, can live in such a condition as would suffocate the strongest man in half an hour? But we thus see how little account we make of the miracles which God works, in consequence of our familiarity with them. The Spirit, therefore, justly rebukes this ingratitude, by commending to our consideration this memorable instance of the grace of God, which is exhibited in our birth and generation.[6]

We now have a very different understanding of the physiology of pregnancy and gestation, but the ways in which two cells continuously divide until they produce a human being is even more astonishing than the understanding of this process that Calvin had in his day. Again, his insight that the more we understand of how the universe works, the more astonished we should be, obtains here as well.

The one challenge we have that Calvin did not confront is how to understand the goodness and love of the Creator in light of the vast suffering and death made inevitable by the process of evolution. Calvin thought that the suffering he saw in all creatures was due to human sin, and that God subjected all creatures to futility in light of the evil that human beings brought into the world (Romans 8:19–22). We now know that the suffering and death that Calvin saw as the ways human sin marred the goodness of God's creation is actually the way God creates. Indeed, we now know that the emergence of life is not possible without suffering and death on an unimaginable scale, as even our own emergence as a species was predicated on the massive dying-off of countless forms of life millions of years ago, to say nothing of the suffering and death of our own biological ancestors. Once again we see that the beauty and terror of the universe are inseparably united, and the terror can no longer be relegated to human sin, but must rather be seen as essential to the way God creates life. However, this should serve to make us all the more humble, when we consider all of the circumstances that had to transpire

---

[6] Comm. Psalm 71:6, CO 31:655–56; CTS 10:85.

for our own lives to emerge, and we should be all the more grateful to those non-human forms of life to which we are inextricably related, as we now can see from the genetic code, and to which we should also be grateful for making our own lives possible. This also means that we cannot follow Calvin in so clearly asserting the distinct superiority of human life when compared to every other form of life. We now know that we exist on an unbroken continuum with all other forms of life, and are vastly inferior to many creatures with regard to many capacities they exhibit in their lives, and are woefully ignorant about the lives of other creatures. We would do better to exhibit a posture of open humility and wonder, being prepared to be continually surprised by all of the wonders that confront us in those we once considered to be dumb beasts who were vastly inferior to us.

We also know that Calvin was not entirely wrong. Because of human activity, we may now be in the midst of one of the greatest die-offs of species in the history of the planet, so that human sin may indeed be responsible for the corruption to which we see so many creatures subjected. Far from contemplating the way God cares for all creatures by providing them food and habitat, as Calvin summoned us to do, we have become utterly careless of the circumstances of other creatures, and view them only as a means to our own flourishing. Our attention only to our own habitat, and our refusal to respect the habitat of the creatures with whom we share this planet, manifests a frightening indifference to the creative work of God, and contradicts the humility and care to which God calls us. On the other hand, if we follow Calvin's lead, we can only applaud and seek to emulate those who study the life and habitat of other creatures, and who call on us to seek their welfare so we might learn to be good neighbors to all creatures, and seek to provide for the flourishing of all life. We can only credibly believe that God cares for us and our lives if we first believe that God cares for all that God has made, including creatures about whom we may never know, and whom we may never see. And we can only believe God cares for them if we also seek to demonstrate our care in whatever ways we can. This should raise for all who believe in the Creator the serious question of whether we should no longer eat our fellow creatures, for the vast number of human beings who inhabit the planet now pose an inexorable threat to all animals below us on the food chain, and our large-scale food production guarantees the suffering and death of countless creatures simply to satisfy our need for food.

Turning to the theme of the second chapter, we have seen that Calvin was aware that the image of God in every person should lead us to see all people in God, so that we love all because we love God. Kierkegaard helps to strengthen this vision of the image of God, by showing how Calvin's other view of the image of God leads inevitably to the creation of alliances, and alliances are the opposite of love for the neighbor. "What the world honors and loves under the name of love is an alliance of self-love."[7] This means that Calvin's other model of love, by which I am drawn to love another by the gifts of God I perceive in the other, is not a model of love after all, but is rather a recipe for the self-love of the alliance, which in Calvin's case is the alliance of the evangelical and orthodox church. Calvin calls our love for others in the church the most sacred bond of union in human life, and even though it does not eradicate the call to love the enemy, it greatly eclipses such love, especially when it is combined with a hope that God will vindicate the godly by striking their enemies with destructive vengeance. Kierkegaard reveals that the church itself constantly succumbs to the temptation to form an alliance, rather than being the place where we learn how to love God, so that we might thereby come to love our neighbor. The problem is especially severe when the church convinces itself that it is precisely by loving one another that we love God. Kierkegaard convincingly shows that when we love one another without having God as the middle term of our love, we are forming an alliance of self-love that

---

[7] Søren Kierkegaard, *Works of Love*, ed. and trans. Howard V. Hong and Edna H. Hong (Princeton University Press, 1995), 119.

excludes the love of God. We can only love others when we first love God, and learn from God what it is to love.

Is it possible to be a member of the Church and not thereby form an alliance of self-love? Does the Church have any positive role in helping people to love God, so that they might thereby learn how to love their neighbor? The first place to begin is with our understanding of Jesus, for if Jesus calls us to form a community united by the most sacred bond of love in Calvin's sense, then Jesus wants us to form an alliance, which makes self-love inevitable. But Kierkegaard points out that Jesus studiously avoids forming any alliances during his life, so that he might be free to love each and every individual whom he encounters.

> He is unconditionally a stranger in the world, without the slightest alliance with anything or with anyone at all in the world, where everything is actually a matter of alliance. It is harder for a rich man to enter the kingdom of heaven than for a camel to go through the eye of a needle, but it is impossible for someone who has even the slightest alliance to serve only one master.[8]

This means that Jesus cannot possibly be calling his followers into an alliance with himself. Rather, he calls them to follow him by serving God alone, by relating directly to God for themselves, each one for himself, and only in that way relating to Jesus and to one another. For Jesus relates first of all to God, and only in that way to his followers. "But then does he indeed have followers? The followers – if they are true followers, there is no alliance, because in relating to the follower he at every moment relates first to God, serving him alone, and if the followers want to create some kind of alliance, then they are not followers."[9]

Jesus calls us to follow him by first of all relating ourselves to God, so that we can learn from God how to love our neighbor, even as

---

[8] Søren Kierkegaard, *"For Self-Examination" and "Judge for Yourself,"* ed. and trans. Howard V. Hong and Edna H. Hong (Princeton University Press, 1990), 170.
[9] Ibid.

Jesus himself provides the prototype of such love to us. This means that each follower of Jesus must devote time and effort to developing his or her relationship to God, in order to learn to love each person individually yet no one exceptionally. Kierkegaard thinks that Jesus gave us the best and most direct way to do this when he told us, "Whenever you pray, go into your room and shut the door and pray to your Father who is in secret" (Matt. 6:6). Even as Jesus consistently withdrew from his followers to pray to God alone, so every follower of Jesus should go into the room, shut the door, and pray to God in solitude. This simple advice actually provides the shortest route to the highest in human life. "Christianity, however, immediately teaches a person the shortest way to find the highest: Shut your door and pray to God – because God surely is the highest."[10] This advice is also the most direct route to finding the neighbor I am to love. Rather than searching for the gifts of God that would draw me to the other person by their goodness, holiness, or beauty, I find my neighbor when I come out of my room after having prayed to God in secret.

> If someone goes out into the world to try to find the beloved or the friend, he can go a long way – and go in vain, can wander the world around – and in vain. But Christianity is never responsible for having a person go even a single step in vain, because when you open the door that you shut in order to pray to God and go out the very first person you meet is the neighbor, whom you *shall* love.[11]

By cultivating our relationship to God in solitary prayer, we learn how to love the neighbor in every individual, for we see ourselves primarily by our relationship with God, and therefore we see the neighbor primarily in light of her relationship to God.

This daily discipline of praying alone in our room with the door shut is also crucial for the development of our own divinely given distinctiveness. Kierkegaard is convinced that every individual has

---

[10] Kierkegaard, *Works of Love*, 51.   [11] Ibid.

a unique vocation from God that each of us can only learn directly from God. "But this I do believe (and I am willing to listen to any objection, but I *will* not believe it), that at every person's birth there comes into existence an eternal purpose for that person, for that person in particular. Faithfulness to oneself with respect to this is the highest thing a person can do."[12] I can only learn my own vocation in life directly from God, and not from any other person. When I go into the room to pray, I am listening to God to learn what it is, who it is, that God is calling me to become. By this practice, I not only learn who I am to become, but I also see that every other individual is to learn from God alone who they are to become, for their vocation is also unique, and is only revealed by God to that individual, as that which constitutes their God-given distinctiveness. "And my task is this: myself an individuality and keeping myself that (and in infinite love God in heaven keeps an eye on this), to proclaim what boundless reality [*Realitet*] every man has in himself when before God he wills to become himself."[13] My love for my neighbor should lead my neighbor into her relationship to God, so that she can learn from God who she is called to become. I love her in her God-given distinctiveness, so that she can develop this distinctiveness in her own relationship to God, when she goes into her room, shuts the door, and prays to God.

What unites us then is not our similarity or difference from one another, for that is the principle of any and every alliance: what unites us is that each of us is relating to God, and relating to one another by means of our relationship to God. The relationship to God also reveals our equality, even in light of our uniqueness, for "every human being (the single individual), unconditionally every human being, once again, unconditionally every human being, is equally

[12] *Upbuilding Discourses in Various Spirits*, ed. and trans. Howard V. and Edna H. Hong (Princeton University Press, 1991), 93.

[13] *Søren Kierkegaard's Journals and Papers*, ed. and trans. Howard V. Hong and Edna H. Hong (Bloomington and London: Indiana University Press, 1975), vol. 6, 535; hereafter references are in the format *Journals and Papers* 6.535.

close to God – how close and equally close? – is loved by him."[14] If I remove the relationship to God, and seek to have the other become an individual by relating to me as an individual, then I am forming an alliance, and I am no longer loving the other person, because I am keeping her from becoming who she is in relation to God. "Act as an individuality yourself, engage a half-dozen Corybants, trumpeters, and drummers to proclaim that one becomes an individuality through a relationship to you – it will work like a charm, will soon become a brilliantly successful business." I can only love my neighbor in her God-given distinctiveness if I first seek to know who I am in relationship to God, so that I can help my neighbor to become who she is in relationship to God, and not by her relationship to me. "Proclaim the truth that every man, unconditionally every man, is an individuality, [and] becomes that by the relationship to God."[15] I am to love my neighbor by helping her to become who she is in relationship to God, so that she can learn to stand alone in relation to God, even as I have learned to stand alone in relation to God. This is where the self-annihilation before God that we discussed in Chapter 5 relates to the love of neighbor, for genuine love helps the other person to stand alone in relation to God, and so in relation to the neighbor I must deny myself, must deny my desire to have the person become who she is in relation to me, so that she can become who she is in relation to God.

> Therefore, giving thanks to God, he declares: Now this individual is standing by himself – through my help. But there is no self-satisfaction in the last phrase, because the loving one has understood that essentially every human being indeed stands by himself – through God's help – and that the loving one's self-annihilation is really only in order not to hinder the other person's God-relationship, so that all the loving one's help infinitely vanishes into the God-relationship.[16]

---

[14] Søren Kierkegaard, *Without Authority*, ed. and trans. Howard V. Hong and Edna H. Hong (Princeton University Press, 1997), 165.
[15] *Journals and Papers* 6.537.   [16] Kierkegaard, *Works of Love*, 278.

The duty to love each and every person in his God-given distinctiveness and equality before God should not be used by Christians as a principle by which to deny the unique relationship of God to the Jews. I have heard many sermons in which Peter's statement that God is not a respecter of persons is taken as a rejection of the Jewish claim to be the elect people of God. God's love for every human being, and our kinship to God by our being created in the image of God, as well as our duty to love our neighbors as ourselves, are primarily revealed through God's election of Israel to be God's chosen people. To his credit, Calvin sees this dynamic very clearly: God's love for us is directly predicated on God's singular love for Israel. The Gospel does not annul the covenant God made with the children of Abraham, but rather joins us to the people of this covenant. Indeed, if the covenant with the Jews is annulled, this would completely undermine any alleged love of God for the Gentiles.

We have tried to give a Christian vision of the election of the Jews based on Calvin's description of the presence of God in Israel, which is a trajectory coming from the exodus and Sinai into the future, rather than from the death and resurrection of Christ into the past. This allows us to see in our own Scripture that the Law of Moses is essentially related to the presence of God in the community, especially after Babylon, as we can see in the figure of Ezra the Scribe. Hence Christians can see the presence of God abiding in the elect people of the Jews, and can understand why they would refuse to abandon the Law for the sake of an alleged saving presence of God in Jesus. Using Calvin, Barth, and Ezra, I have sought to create a Christian foundation by which the Jews may be seen as the one elect people of God before and after Jesus and Paul, whose presence in our midst is a living monument to the abiding love and faithfulness of God. This will allow Christians to listen in openness to their Jewish brothers and sisters, so that we can learn from them how they understand their election and their unique relationship with God.

The question that remains unresolved is how to portray the continuity of Jesus and Paul to the restoration of the Jews after Babylon.

To his great credit, Calvin places this issue squarely before us, for he essentially links the restoration of the Jews after Babylon to the coming of Christ. Calvin does this by focusing on the Temple and its sacrifices, which he sees as fulfilled and therefore terminated in the death of Christ. If we attend to Ezra and the role of the Law in the restoration of the Jews, then we can certainly see why the Jewish tradition follows the trajectory it does, including the development of the Rabbinic schools of thought, but then it is increasingly difficult to see how Jesus and Paul can be in any kind of continuity with this restoration. Indeed, Paul's claims that the law is a ministry of condemnation and death, and his willingness to regard the law as refuse for the sake of Christ, would be a direct threat to the restoration of the Jews after Ezra.

One way by which this issue might be addressed would be to see Jesus as primarily concerned with the Jews who were excluded from full membership in the community by their living outside the law as sinners. Jesus explicitly claims to be sent to this group in particular. When his disciples were asked why their teacher ate with tax collectors and sinners, Jesus responded by saying, "Those who are well have no need of a physician, but those who are sick. Go and learn what this means, 'I desire mercy, not sacrifice.' For I have come not to call the righteous but sinners" (Matt. 9:12–13). In this statement, Jesus describes the righteous, those who live by the law of God revealed to Moses, as well, and states that he has not come for them, but for the sick, for tax collectors and sinners who are not living by the law of Moses. This has often been taken to mean that Jesus is against the righteous, as though his coming for the sick meant that he was rejecting those who were well. But it is clear from this statement, as well as from his parables, that Jesus regarded the righteous as safely within the fold of the kingdom, as those who are already cared for by the shepherd of Israel. Jesus is interested in the lost sheep of the house of Israel (Matt. 10:6), but he does not mean to cast out the sheep who are not lost. After all, Jesus eats with Pharisees as well as tax collectors, and he heals the daughter of the leader of the synagogue, even as he also heals the slave of a centurion. More importantly, even though the elder son does not rejoice when his lost brother is found, his father does not withdraw his love from him or cast him out of the family. Rather, he assures him, "Son, you are always with me, and all that is mine is yours" (Luke 15:31). Similarly, the shepherd rejoices when the one lost sheep is found, but this does not deny the fact that the other ninety-nine were not lost (Luke 15:3–7). So Jesus assumes that the righteous already belong to the family of God, which is why he is so passionately interested in those who are excluded from the community by their being sinners. Jesus is dismayed by the lack of mercy being shown to tax collectors and sinners by the righteous, and so he places them ahead of the righteous in terms of their inheritance of the kingdom of heaven. But the righteous also inherit the kingdom, just behind the tax collectors and sinners. "Truly, I tell you, the tax collectors and prostitutes are going into the kingdom of heaven ahead of you" (Matt. 21:31).

This is not to deny that Jesus comes into direct conflict with the righteous owing to his willingness to see tax collectors, prostitutes, and sinners as heirs of the kingdom of God and legitimate members of the covenant community. This leads to many of the statements in which it sounds like the righteous will be cast out of the kingdom of heaven, because of their rejection of Jesus and his followers (Matt. 21:43). However, this does not change the central dynamic at work in the ministry of Jesus, at least in this view, which is that the love of God for the righteous Jews is radiating out through Jesus to the Jews who are condemned by the law, and who were seen to be excluded from the love of God for God's chosen people. Jesus can then be seen as seeking to complete the restoration begun by Ezra and the Scribes, as he seeks to restore to the fold the lost sheep of the house of Israel, who could not be restored by the law.

The message of Jesus and his followers has always resonated more clearly in the community outside of the law, initially among the lost sheep of the house of Israel, and then even more explosively among the Gentiles. The rejection of Jesus and his Gospel by the righteous

Jews provoked a strong reaction among the followers of Jesus, including Paul, who initially thought that such rejection placed these Jews under the wrath of God. "Thus they have constantly been filling up the measure of their sins; but God's wrath has overtaken them at last" (1 Thess. 2:16). However, Paul also knows what Calvin came to know from him, that the Jews can never be rejected by God, for God's love for Israel is now radiating out from Israel to the Gentiles through the Gospel Paul preaches. Hence he warns the Gentiles not to despise the Jews who reject the Gospel. "If you do boast, remember that it is not you that support the root, but the root that supports you" (Romans 11:18). Those who can be seen as enemies of God by their rejection of the Gospel must be seen as beloved by God for the sake of their ancestors, "for the gifts and the calling of God are irrevocable" (Romans 11:29).

The task now is to move beyond even this remarkable statement of Paul, and see the Jews as always being beloved of God for the sake of their ancestors, for the sake of the irrevocable covenant God has made with them. This will allow us to appreciate the centrality of Exodus and Sinai for the Jewish people, for these are the ways by which they were claimed totally and completely by the love of God. We may believe that God's passionate love for the Jews has now radiated out in the Gospel of Jesus Christ to include the lost sheep of the house of Israel, as well as the Gentiles; but the heart of this love is revealed in Exodus and Sinai, as those events are celebrated and lived in the Jewish community. Calvin himself saw how the Exodus was a singular pledge of the love of God for the children of Abraham, one that was binding for all generations; and he also came to see how even Sinai itself, with its amazing display of the glory of God, is also a perpetual pledge of God's singular love for the Israelites.

For why did God appear upon that occasion in such a glorious manner? Evidently to show that his covenant formed a sacred bond of union between him and the posterity of Abraham. Hence the words of Moses – "Say not in thine heart, Who shall go up into heaven?

Or who shall descend into the deep? Or who shall go over the sea? For the word is nigh unto thee ..." (Deut. 30:12). Sinai accordingly is mentioned by David, to teach us that if we would fortify our minds with a firm faith in the Divine presence, we must derive it from the Law and the Prophets.[17]

With regard to the knowledge of ourselves, we have seen that Calvin is profoundly aware of how easy it is to deceive ourselves about ourselves, and sought to lead us on the right path to the knowledge of ourselves. One of the most pervasive ways we deceive ourselves is by comparing ourselves with others. Hence the only way by which we might be revealed to ourselves is to be summoned alone before God, so that we might learn to see ourselves in conscience the way God already sees us. Calvin thought that this was why David so often speaks of communing with himself on his bed, for the silence and solitude of the night allows him to see himself more accurately than when he is in the presence of others during the day.

> We know that, during our intercourse with men in the day time, our thoughts are distracted, and we often judge rashly, being deceived by the external appearance; whereas in solitude, we can give to any subject a closer attention; and, farther, the sense of shame does not then hinder a man from thinking without disguise of his own faults. David, therefore, exhorts his enemies to withdraw from those who witnessed and judged of their actions on the public stage of life, and to be alone, that they may examine themselves more truthfully and honestly. And this exhortation has a respect to us all; for there is nothing to which men are more prone than to deceive one another with empty applause, until each man enter into himself, and commune alone with his own heart.[18]

---

[17] Comm. Psalm 68:17, CO 31:627A; CTS 10:24. I am indebted to Yehuda Gellman for his insight into the way the love of God overwhelms the Jews in Exodus and Sinai, in a way which is *sui generis*, even as this love may radiate out from the Jews to all people.

[18] Comm. Psalm 4:5, CO 31:61–62; CTS 8:44.

This examination of ourselves at night is directly related to the purpose of prayer for Calvin, which is that God may be the witness of all our affections.[19] We are more likely to reveal all of our affections to God in prayer at night, for the presence of others might hinder this disclosure owing to our sense of shame arising from the sins of which our conscience makes us aware.

> The time when he declares God to have visited him is during *the night*, because, when a man is withdrawn from the presence of his fellow-creatures, he sees more clearly his sins, which otherwise would be hidden from his view; just as, on the contrary, the sight of men affects us with shame, and this is, as it were, a veil before our eyes, which prevents us from deliberately examining our faults. It is, therefore, as if David had said, O Lord, since the darkness of the night discovers the conscience more fully, all coverings being then taken away, and since, at that season, the affections, either good or bad, according to men's inclinations, manifest themselves more freely, when there is no person present to witness and pronounce judgment upon them; if thou then examinest me, there will be found neither disguise nor deceit in my heart.[20]

We come truly to know ourselves when we pray in secret at night, for then we make God alone the witness of our affections, without any concern for what others might think. Hence by praying to God in solitude, we can begin to escape the self-deception of hypocrisy, and bring ourselves alone into the presence of God.

> It is when we hold converse with him apart, and with no human eye to witness us, that we feel the vanity of hypocrisy, and will be likely to utter only what we have well and seriously meditated in our hearts. Nothing tends more to beget a reverential awe of God upon our spirits than bringing ourselves before his face.[21]

[19] Comm. Psalm 10:13, CO 31:116B; CTS 8:150.
[20] Comm. Psalm 17:3, CO 31:160B; CTS 8:238.
[21] Comm. Psalm 66:3, CO 31:611A; CTS 9:467.

6

CONCLUSION

Such silence and solitude is also essential to the task of discerning and hearing the voice of conscience. As Kierkegaard points out, the fastest way to silence the voice of conscience is always to be part of a group.

> It could be said that "conscience" is one of life's greatest inconveniences. Therefore, "Let's be part of a group," for if we are part of a group it means good-night to conscience. We cannot be two or three, a Miller Brothers and Company around conscience. Let's make all this coziness secure by abolishing conscience, by saying that wanting to be a single individual is egotism, morbid vanity, etc.[22]

This means that Kierkegaard does not see the abolition of conscience manifesting itself in the malicious who commit evil without any sense of restraint, but rather in the cultured citizens of his day who seek to make themselves into something solely by comparison to the criteria set by the members of their group or alliance. "Of course, a lack of conscience does not manifest itself as criminal acts – which would be stupid, foolish, and ill-advised – no, no, it manifests itself with moderation, to a certain degree, and then with taste and culture; it makes life cozy and enjoyable – but yet is it not too much to make it into earnestness and culture!"[23] Like Calvin, Kierkegaard assumes that every person has a conscience, for without conscience we cannot know ourselves, nor can we hear the summons to stand alone before God as the distinctive individuals we are. However, Kierkegaard is even more aware than Calvin how difficult it is to develop a conscience, so that we hear its voice. "It is presupposed and stated that every human being has a conscience – yet there is no accomplishment (neither in the physical, like dancing or singing, nor in the mental, such as thinking and the like) which requires such an extensive and rigorous schooling as is required before one can genuinely be said to have a conscience."[24] This is why Kierkegaard

[22] *Journals and Papers* 2:417.
[23] Søren Kierkegaard, *"For Self-Examination" and "Judge for Yourself"*, 40.
[24] *Journals and Papers* 1:321.

exhorts us to go into our room, close the door, and pray to God; for in the silence and solitude of prayer, we might begin to hear and develop the voice of conscience.

The voice of conscience is known when I hear the question it poses to me about myself. "There, where there is *no one* who asks and where there is nevertheless a personal question, an invisible one is there, the questioner; there in the deepest sense *you* are involved with yourself, and this is the relationship of conscience."[25] Once I hear the voice of conscience, I hear the voice of eternity questioning me solely about myself.

> But who is it indeed who is asking the question? No one, no one! Yet you know very well that the most terrible, the most earnest question is the one of which it must be said: There is no one who is asking the question, and yet there is a question – and a question to you *personally*. If that is the case, then it is the conscience that is asking the question.[26]

This voice, which poses to me the question about myself, can only be answered by me, and thus it makes me completely responsible for myself, taking all my attention away from others: "you come to feel the full weight of the truth that it is you who alone are assigned to yourself, have nothing, nothing at all, to do with others, but have all the more, or rather, everything to do with yourself."[27] I have only to do with myself, I am completely responsible for myself, I alone, in a way that includes the way I respond to what others do in relation to me. "You have to do only with what you do unto others, or how you take what others do unto you. The direction is inward; essentially you have to do only with yourself before God."[28] As the question of conscience is addressed solely to me, and to no one else, so its question can only be answered by me, and by no one else. "But in eternity

25 Søren Kierkegaard, *Christian Discourses*, ed. and trans. Howard V. Hong and Edna H. Hong (Princeton University Press, 1997), 236.
26 Ibid., 236.   27 Ibid., 238.   28 Kierkegaard, *Works of Love*, 384.

you are a single individual, and conscience, when it speaks with you, is no third person, no more than you are a third person when you are speaking with the conscience, because you and the conscience are one; it knows everything you know, and it knows that you know it."[29] If what I know is related to what I read in Scripture, then conscience immediately refers what I know to myself, and poses it as a question to my life. It does not allow me to use what I know as a weapon by which to judge or shame others, it poses what I know as a question to myself alone, asking me to what degree my life expresses what I have come to know.

> To be alone with Holy Scripture! I dare not! If I open it – any passage – it traps me at once; it asks me (indeed, it is as if it were God himself who asked me): Have you done what you read there? And then, then – yes, I am trapped. Then either straight away into action – or immediately a humbling admission.[30]

Since conscience knows what I know, and knows that I know it, it makes me transparent before myself, even when what I see contradicts what I know (as it always will before the requirements of God in Scripture); and the more transparent I become to myself in conscience, the more I become the person God has created me to become.

> And a man's salvation lies precisely in his becoming a person. Yes, this rule could be formulated: One who becomes a personality, one who succeeds in coming that far, or who comes that far, ordinarily is saved. Why? Because he is so transparent that he cannot hide from himself – yes, illuminated as if he were transparent.[31]

The voice of conscience also echoes and reinforces what Kierkegaard calls "the echo of eternity," by which the judgment

---

[29] *Upbuilding Discourses in Various Spirits*, 131.
[30] Kierkegaard, *"For Self-Examination" and "Judge for Yourself,"* 31.
[31] *Journals and Papers* 3:488.

I make regarding others becomes the judgment eternity will make regarding me. "But the Christian like for like is: God will do unto you exactly as you do unto others."[32] Conscience reveals to me that I cannot have a private relationship with God, in which I invoke God to be the Judge of my neighbor, while I myself remain exempt from judgment. Jesus tells us as much quite clearly. "Do not judge, so that you may not be judged. For with the judgment you make you will be judged, and the measure you give will be the measure you get" (Matt. 7:1–2). I am not responsible for what others do to me, but I am completely responsible for how I respond to what others do, and if I respond by casting judgment on them, then the judgment I give will be the judgment I receive. This is where Calvin's interest in summoning the judgment of God upon his enemies is especially problematic. How can I not judge my enemy, when I am confident that God both judges and condemns my enemy? How am I to love my enemy, if I am convinced that God eternally hates my enemy, and seeks to destroy my enemy, because my enemy is God's enemy? How can I forgive those who wrong me, if I place all my hope in their being held fully accountable by God? If Kierkegaard is right, and if Jesus is right, then when I cease to hope for the salvation of another, I lose hope of my own salvation as well.

> In the same degree to which he hopes for others, he hopes for himself, because in the very same degree to which he hopes for others, he is the one who loves. And in the very same degree to which he hopes for others, he hopes for himself, because this is the infinitely accurate, the eternal like for like, that is in everything eternal.[33]

Thus I must never cease to hope for others, no matter how evil and hopeless they may seem to me; I must never cease to love my enemy, no matter how betrayed I might feel, especially if my enemy had been my friend. To the same degree I have hope for myself, I must

[32] Kierkegaard, *Works of Love*, 383.   [33] Ibid., 255.

have hope for all others; and to the same degree I have hope for everyone else, I have hope for myself.

> Therefore never unlovingly give up on any human being or give up hope for that person, since it is possible that even the most prodigal son could still be saved, that even the most embittered enemy – alas, he who was your friend – it is still possible that he could again become your friend. It is possible that the one who sank the deepest – alas, because he stood so high – it is still possible that he could be raised up. It is still possible that the love that became cold could again begin to burn. Therefore never give up on any human being; do not despair, not even at the last moment – no, hope all things.[34]

This is very different than the way Calvin would have us regard our enemies. Though we should hold out hope for them, that they may yet be converted, we hold out the equal possibility that they may be reprobate, and hence devoted to destruction by the vengeance of God. If the latter is the case, then we may rightly rejoice when we see the vengeance of God exhibited against them, as much as we would rejoice in their (now lost) salvation. "On the other hand, when one is led by a holy zeal to sympathize with the justness of that vengeance which God may have inflicted, his joy will be as pure in beholding the retribution of the wicked, as his desire for their conversion and salvation was strong and unfeigned."[35] In this sense, Calvin claims that one may even pray for the destruction of one's enemies, provided that one does so under the guidance of the wisdom, uprightness, and moderation of the Holy Spirit. "We need wisdom by which to distinguish between those who are wholly reprobate and those of whose amendment there is still some hope; we have also need of uprightness, that none may devote himself exclusively to his own private interests; and of moderation too, to dispose our minds to calm endurance."[36] So long as we pray in this way, and not out of the

---

[34] Ibid., 254.   [35] Comm. Psalm 58:10, CO 31:563B; CTS 9:378.
[36] Comm. Psalm 69:22, CO 31:647B; CTS 10:67.

passion of personal revenge, Calvin says that we may call on God to manifest his vengeance against our enemies, even if they had been our friends, even if they were members of our Church.

> As then David desires that the vengeance of God may be manifested, he very properly speaks of the reprobation of his enemies in language accommodated to our understanding; as if he had said, O God! reckon them not among the number or ranks of thy people, and let them not be gathered together with thy Church; but rather show by destroying them that thou hast rejected them; and although they occupy a place for a time among thy faithful ones, do thou at length cut them off, to make it manifest that they were aliens, though they were mingled with the members of thy family.[37]

Calvin sees no spiritual danger in such prayers, as though this would not at all affect our ability to love those who hate us, to bless those who curse us, and to pray for those who persecute us. Instead, he claims that they come from a holy zeal inspired in us by the Holy Spirit.

And it must be admitted that this is not simply Calvin's problem. The issue of praying for the manifestation of the vengeance of God against our enemies arises in the Psalms themselves, which have been central to Christian worship throughout the history of the Church, and which were especially important to Calvin. Calvin thought that we must be able to pray using the words of the Psalms, for they were inspired by the Holy Spirit, and used by the same covenant community of which we are now members. Calvin tries his best to make sure that the godly do not use such prayers as an excuse to foster their own desire for personal revenge. David's "example cannot justly be pleaded in self-vindication by those who pour forth their wrath and spite upon every one that comes in their way, or who are carried away by a foolish impatience to take revenge; never allowing themselves to reflect for a moment what good purpose this

---

[37] Comm. Psalm 69:28, CO 31:650B; CTS 10:74.

can serve, nor making any efforts to keep their passion within due bounds."[38] The "holy zeal" by which these prayers may rightly be spoken is guided by the Holy Spirit, and thus focuses on the justice of God's cause in the Church, and not the settling of personal scores with our enemies. Nonetheless, Calvin claims that the manifestation of God's vengeance on our enemies is the sole comfort of the godly in their affliction, and it is this for which we pray, making it hard to see how to harmonize such prayers with loving, blessing, praying for, and forgiving our enemies.

Nor is this a problem only for the Hebrew Scriptures. The same New Testament which begins with the command of Jesus to love our enemies and forgive those who wrong us ends with the cry of the martyrs for vengeance. "Sovereign Lord, holy and true, how long will it be before you judge and avenge our blood on the inhabitants of the earth?" (Rev. 6:10). Their cry is heard and answered by the Lamb who was slain, and their enemies "will also drink the wine of God's wrath, poured unmixed into the cup of his anger, and they will be tormented with fire and sulfur in the presence of the holy angels and in the presence of the Lamb. And the smoke of their torment goes up forever and ever" (Rev. 14:10–11). The Pauline author also tells the Thessalonians to look forward to the day when the Lord Jesus Christ will come with vengeance to repay with eternal destruction those who have afflicted them.

> For it is indeed just of God to repay with affliction those who afflict you, and to give relief to the afflicted as well as to us, when the Lord Jesus is revealed from heaven with his mighty angels in flaming fire, inflicting vengeance on those who do not obey the gospel of our Lord Jesus. These will suffer the punishment of eternal destruction, separated from the presence of the Lord and the glory of his might, when he comes to be glorified by his saints and to be marveled at on that day among all who have believed, because our testimony to you was believed. (2 Thess. 1:6–10)

[38] Comm. Psalm 69:22, CO 31:647B; CTS 10:67.

This is why the visions of Julian are so remarkable, for she knew that these passages are present in the Word of God, and are taught by Holy Church, but when she looked at what God was showing her, she saw no anger in God, no vengeance in God, no wrath in God.

> For this is what was shown: that our life is all rooted and grounded in love, and without love we cannot live; and therefore to the soul which through God's special grace sees so much of his great and marvelous goodness, and sees that we are joined to him in love forever, it is the greatest impossibility conceivable that God should be angry.[39]

Were there anger in God, then God would render evil for evil, as would be the case were God to show vengeance toward our enemies. However, Julian is reminded that God is the one who creates good out of evil, for this is the very nature of God, revealed when God brought the greatest good in Christ out of the greatest evil in Adam. "So what our blessed Lord's teaching means is that we should take heed of the following: 'Since I have turned the greatest possible harm into good, it is my will that you should know from this that I shall turn all lesser evil into good.'"[40] Since the love of God brings great good out of great evil, when we come to know this love, it wears away our anger, which only wants to render evil for evil. Julian comes to see that "the effect of God's mercy and forgiveness is to lessen and wear away our anger."[41] This could not happen were there truly anger in God.

Does this then mean that there is no place for anger in the Christian life? Can the Christian help becoming angry when she is unjustly afflicted or oppressed by others, or when she sees the brutal suffering of those she loves at the hands of their enemies? There is no doubt in my mind that such anger is a natural human response to such events, and it would be foolish and self-defeating to try

---

[39] Julian of Norwich, *Revelations of Divine Love*, trans. Elizabeth Spearing (London: Penguin Books, 1998), 112.
[40] Ibid., 82.　[41] Ibid., 111.

to suppress this anger before it even arises. But the question then becomes, what do we do once we are angry? Do those who anger us cease to exist for us, so that we no longer exist for them, but only for those they have harmed? Do we ask God to become the agent of our righteous anger, and pray for God to show vengeance to those who have wronged us, since what angers us must definitely anger God?

Julian tells us that when we turn to God in prayer, we will not find one who will infinitize our anger, but rather one who forgives us even in the midst of our anger, and who therefore wears away our anger, making it possible for us to love again, to hope again, and to forgive again. She also reminds us that our anger is the greatest threat not to our enemies, but to ourselves. For if my deepest desire is to make God into the infinite agent of my anger, I will always and only succeed in bringing God's anger upon myself. This is something Kierkegaard saw quite clearly in light of Jesus' commandment not to judge lest we be judged. "If you refuse to forgive, then you actually want something else: you want to make God hard-hearted so that he, too, would not forgive – how then could this hard-hearted God forgive you? If you cannot bear other people's faults against you, how then should God be able to bear yours against him?"[42] This again is why we need solitude, for in the solitude I can actually begin to hear the way the judgments that I make about others directly echo back to myself. "If you have never been solitary, then you have never discovered that God is. But if you have been truly solitary, then you have also learned that God just repeats everything you say and do to other people; he repeats it with the magnification of infinity."[43] Thus when we bring our anger to God, and ask God to show anger to those who have wronged us, we not only increase the anger within us, but also invoke the anger of God upon ourselves. "God is actually himself the pure like for like, the pure rendition of how you yourself are. If there is anger in you, then God is anger in you; if there is leniency and mercifulness in you, then God is mercifulness in you."[44]

---

[42] Kierkegaard, *Works of Love*, 384.   [43] Ibid.   [44] Ibid.

But if God is love, and is the eternal spring of love flowing into every human heart, then when we are angry, we should pray to God to melt this anger in our hearts, so that love may freely flow again, this time towards those who have injured or wronged us.

> It must needs be that the one who wears away and extinguishes our anger and makes us gentle and kind is himself always consistently loving and kind, which is the contrary of anger, for I saw quite clearly that where our Lord appears, everything is peaceful and there is no place for anger, for I saw no kind of anger in God.[45]

Jesus turns us directly toward those who anger us, and commands us to pray for them, to bless them, to forgive them, to love them. He does not allow us to cease existing for them, but commands us to exist for them in the same way we are to exist for every other individual. Thus, when we become understandably angry by what our enemies have done, we should bring our enemies directly before God in our prayer, asking for the strength to bless them, to forgive them, to love them. This should be part of our daily discipline when we shut the door to pray to God in secret.

So we are left with a choice. Do we hold to the visions of destructive vengeance, teaching us to rejoice in the eternal destruction of our enemies, as those are found throughout Scripture? Or do we follow Julian, and hold that in spite of these visions, there is no anger, no blame, no vengeance in God, which makes it possible for us to be freed of our anger, so that we can forgive those who wrong us, love those who hate us, bless those who curse us, pray for those who persecute us? Do we dare to lose hope for our enemies, knowing that by doing so we may well lose hope for ourselves? Or do we out of love hope all things for everyone, knowing that only in this way can we have any hope?

[45] Julian of Norwich, *Revelations of Divine Love*, 112.

Index

INDEX